REDUCING URBAN UNEMPLOYMENT

WHAT WORKS AT THE LOCAL LEVEL

William H. McCarthy

with

David R. Jones

R. Leo Penne

Lucy R. Watkins

National League of Cities

October 1985

Orders for this publication should be sent
to:

Publication Sales
National League of Cities
1301 Pennsylvania Avenue, N.W.
Washington, D.C. 20004

Price: $10 for NLC Direct Member Cities;
$15 for all others. Please add
$2 for postage and handling.

CONTENTS

Chapter 5

DISLOCATED WORKERS

PREFACE

For most Americans the term "unemployment" is a statistic which refers to the collective job-related problems of others. And while most of us go through changes in jobs and sometimes even careers during our working lives, our skills and experiences usually lead to new and better positions.

However, for as many as 13 million Americans, "unemployment" means something quite different. For roughly 11 percent of the workforce, the term refers to the difficulties and despair of being unable to obtain or hold a job for a wide variety of reasons. When experienced for prolonged periods, unemployment, for many, means being confined to living in poverty without the key to getting out.

Perhaps the most vulnerable of all groups to the effects of unemployment is disadvantaged youth. To this group, unemployment represents an inability to obtain jobs—particularly full-time jobs—due to deficiencies in basic skills, lack of experience and ignorance of how to find a job. The effects of these barriers to youth employment combine to form a pattern of disadvantage—a pattern characterized by poor job opportunities, low earnings and, typically, chronic unemployment.

This pattern of disadvantage brought on by unemployment and related problems has a way, all too predictably, of following youth into their adult years. For single women with children, especially those who become parents as teenagers and do so at the cost of their own educational and skill development, the difficulties of finding and keeping a job are often insurmountable. Among other groups of adults, a lack of marketable skills, poor employment histories and personal problems create barriers to work which result in long-term unemployment, underemployment and circumstances in which individuals are discouraged from even seeking a job.

Another group of adult workers today faces serious employment-related problems. For this group, known as "dislocated" or "displaced" workers, problems differ in that they do not result from a lack of skills, experience or the presence of personal problems, but rather from the disappearance of jobs for which their skills were once in demand. Frequently in the middle of their careers or beyond, dislocated workers typically have deep roots where they live and are thus less likely to move where new jobs can be found. Some are also reluctant to retrain for new occupations, at least in part because many dislocated workers will earn less in their new jobs than in the ones from which they were displaced.

For the individuals and families affected personally by problems related to unemployment, the stakes are high. They are also high for the rest of society, and the point where these problems have their most jarring social impact is at the local community level.

The elected officials of local government have a particular concern with the causes and consequences of unemployment. For them, unemployment is not experienced as a national statistic, nor is it felt only in terms of human hardship within their local community. It is also a problem with social, economic and fiscal dimensions that are the substance of their daily policy concerns as local government officials.

People without income can't consume locally-produced goods and services.

Those without jobs can't pay local taxes. And yet, their need for public goods and services does not decline. If anything, unemployment causes them to increase. The unemployed can't adequately house themselves and their families. They and their dependents often suffer from inadequate health care. Their children experience difficulties in school. Prolonged periods of unemployment are associated with a whole series of social and economic needs which manifest themselves as public policy issues and fiscal problems for local government officials.

In August 1984, the National League of Cities surveyed officials to determine their views on the unemployment situation in their own city. Twenty percent of those who responded described local unemployment as a "top priority" problem and an additional 42 percent described it as a "high priority" matter in their community. This sense of importance was shared by municipal officials in all regions of the country and from cities of all sizes. Perhaps even more striking, most of these officials saw local unemployment problems as likely to persist into the forseeable future.

Reducing Urban Unemployment: What Works at the Local Level is, in part, a book about the types of employment-related problems faced by America's cities. More important, it is a book about what cities, as communities, are doing to ameliorate those problems, with insights into how others might do so as well.

The book, which features twenty-one case studies of local initiatives to reduce unemployment, results from the interest of the National League of Cities and, in particular, the League's 1984 Task Force on Urban Unemployment, in sharing among cities ideas and examples of what is working in a variety of communities across the country. Its intended audience is the wide group of institutions, organizations and individuals who share a stake in reducing the incidence and effects of urban unemployment. This audience includes elected officials, employment and training professionals, educators, business leaders, community-based organizations and philanthropies.

Readers of this book will observe, in case study after case study, that successful local initiatives to reduce unemployment involve—if not require—working partnerships as wide and diverse as the audience for which it is written.

The principal author and editor of Reducing Urban Unemployment: What Works at the Local Level, is William H. McCarthy. Mr. McCarthy is a Policy Analyst with the National League of Cities' Office of Policy Analysis and Development. He has responsibility for a range of human development issues of which employment is one. The author is a former local elected official from Massachusetts and holds a Bachelor of Arts Degree in Urban Studies/Political Science from Columbia University.

William E. Davis, III
Director,
Office of Policy Analysis
and Development
National League of Cities

ACKNOWLEDGMENTS

REDUCING URBAN UNEMPLOYMENT: What Works At The Local Level owes its origins to the group of thirty-five local elected officials who served on the National League of Cities' 1984 Urban Unemployment Task Force. The Task Force, chaired by Mayor Donald Fraser of Minneapolis, considered the problem of joblessness in America's cities from a variety of perspectives, identified the groups of urban residents most affected by the problem and studied successful local initiatives to reduce it. As a means of sharing their findings, Task Force members expressed the wish to have a sourcebook of successful local efforts produced for dissemination among city officials, employment and training professionals and others interested in its subject. As staffperson to the Task Force and later a guide in the development of this project, William R. Barnes, Director for Research with NLC's Office of Policy Analysis and Development, is acknowledged for his valuable contributions.

NLC wishes to acknowledge the special contributions of three individuals to the research and production of this book. Lucy R. Watkins, Consultant to the Roosevelt Centennial Youth Project, with the help of the Project's Director, Frank J. Slobig, researched and drafted the case studies which address the problems of disadvantaged youth. David R. Jones, a free-lance Washington, D.C. writer, researched and drafted the case studies on hard-to-employ adult programs. And R. Leo Penne, a free-lance Washington consultant and writer, provided research and drafted case studies on local efforts to assist dislocated workers. The contributions and efforts of these individuals are deeply appreciated.

NLC's Director of the Office of Policy Analysis and Development, William E. Davis III, played a valuable role in contributing ideas and editorial assistance, as well as in guiding the progress of the project.

The production and administrative support of NLC's Althea L. Ray, Lesley-Ann Rennie and Deborah E. Johnson, as well as the manuscript typing assistance of Daryl Sargeant are also deeply appreciated.

Lastly, NLC wishes to express its thanks to the many local officials and program staff whose input into the research and preparation of the twenty-one case studies have made this book a hopeful contributor to reducing urban unemployment.

William H. McCarthy

Chapter 1

URBAN UNEMPLOYMENT
The Problem

URBAN UNEMPLOYMENT
The Problem

At the outset, a discussion of urban unemployment raises the question of whether, in a general sense, unemployment differs in its effects on urban and non-urban areas of the country. The answer is both no and yes.

On one hand, in its nature and manifestations, the problem of unemployment in cities is not generally different from the problem in small towns, suburbs or the nation as a whole. On the other, the concentration of nearly three-quarters of the U.S. population[1] in urban areas—with densities in central cities fifty-five times the national average—suggests, at a minimum, that concentrations of problems such as unemployment are greater in urban areas. When factors such as higher incidence of poverty, crime, overcrowded schools and decaying economic bases are considered, the difference between urban unemployment and any other form of the problem becomes one of *magnitude*.

Comprehending the magnitude of unemployment in cities requires some understanding of the nature of the problem in general, its dimensions, and its impacts on specific segments of the population. The following sections of this chapter address these aspects of unemployment, with a concluding section assessing their impact at the local level.

The Complex Nature of Unemployment

The term "unemployment" refers not to a single problem but to a multiplicity of problems: some personal, some social, others economic and still others political in nature. While interrelated, and often compound in their effects on individuals, groups, communities and the nation as a whole, the causes of these multiple problems are, at some level, separable. Thus, solutions to "unemployment," if they are to address more than a single element of a complex set of problems, must necessarily be comprehensive and, at the same time, flexible in order to deal with the differing types and degrees of employment-related problems.

Classifying Unemployment Problems

The wide range of problems which can be regarded as "employment-related" can be grouped into two general classifications. One, encompassing a host of barriers, impediments, deficiencies, etc., which prevent one's finding or inhibit one's keeping a job, can be labeled "employability problems." The other, emanating from forces, trends and cycles within the economy which influence the types and availability of jobs, can be labeled "opportunity problems." Grouped into this second classification also are the special opportunity problems encountered through discrimination within the labor economy—on account of race, age, sex, handicap etc.—though, arguably, the bases of discrimination represent employablity problems as well.

Employability Problems

While the effects of barriers to employment have differing effects on different segments of the workforce, e.g., youth, adults and older workers, there are commonalities in the types of barriers which present employability problems. Four types of barriers, varying in degree and combinations, are generally responsible for such problems:

3

- **Basic Educational Deficiencies**—more and more, the inadequacies of fundamental reading, writing and computational skills are distancing workers—of all ages—from available jobs in in-demand occupations.

- **Lack of Basic Job Skills**—with unemployment often tied to educational deficiencies, unskilled workers find themselves in a Catch-22 situation in which they cannot gain skills without experience, but cannot gain experience without requisite skills to obtain jobs.

- **Mismatch of Skills and In-demand Jobs**—more a characteristic of older and/or dislocated workers, this barrier often negates years of experience in jobs for which there is no longer a demand and skills which are not easily transferrable to new occupations.

- **Miscellaneous Barriers**—such as teenage parenthood, language difficulties, behavioral problems, and various forms of handicaps.

Most alarming about these barriers to employability is that, within certain segments of the population and within certain demographic areas of the country—most notably inner cities and rural areas—they are all present in high degrees producing formidable combinations. From the perspective of employment and training professionals, the challenge to eliminate such complex barriers is a long and arduous one, one in which success is frequently measured in increments rather than bottom lines.

Opportunity Problems

Different in nature from employability problems, opportunity problems result chiefly from factors extrinsic to workers and their characteristics. Of these factors, the economy—more specifically, changes and fluctuations within the economy—is dominant in its contribution to labor market shifts which produce opportunities for some and problems for others. The term "opportunity problems" is used here to refer to individuals in the latter circumstance.

Problems which affect the numbers and types of employment opportunities can be divided into four sub-categories. As in the case of employability problems, each of the four have varying effects on youth, adults and older workers. They are:

- **Insufficient Number of Jobs**—the broadest of employability problems, "insufficiency," in absolute terms, is an ever-present circumstance. As a fundamental factor in unemployment levels, it is a product of changes within the economy and, increasingly, of the exportation of production and, hence, jobs. In this respect, it is tied to another, more specific opportunity problem—occupational/industry decline.

- **Occupational/Industry Decline**—the primary factor in the evolution of the "dislocated worker" phenomenon, the general decline of the U.S. manufacturing economy and acute declines in certain industries have shrunk the U.S. labor market by more than 11 million jobs between 1979 and 1983 alone.[2] No longer a "rustbelt" versus "sunbelt" issue, dislocation or displacement, as the problem is also known, today spares not a single state or region of the country. While finite product life spans and inevitable changes in consumer demands account for some decline, overseas production by "American" companies and importation of foreign-made goods are major contributors.

■ Disparities in Labor Force Skills and Job Market Demand—an opportunity problem subdivided into two problems: one, the incongruence of many workers' skills and current demands for skilled labor; and two, the overall shortage of skilled labor which, in many parts of the country, retards economic development potential and opportunities for job creation. In concert, these disparities not only deprive workers of opportunities for economic self-sufficiency, they also inhibit the economic growth of the nation as a whole.

■ Discrimination in the Workplace—the most insidious of opportunity problems, discrimination is practiced both consciously and in a *de facto* sense through hiring patterns, locational decisions and compensation practices. Its practice disproportionately affects the poor, women, minorities, younger and older workers and the handicapped, many of whom share common characteristics, including urban residency.

As causes and explanations of the nature of unemployment, employability and opportunity problems suggest the symptoms of what may be regarded as a human resource "disease." While various remedies or cures for the disease do exist in the forms of education and remediation, occupational and skill training and retraining, job creations and enforcement of equal opportunity laws, they are dispensable largely on an individual case basis, consequently ensuring limits on the numbers of "remedied" or "cured" problems. The broad manifestations of the disease, i.e.,

the different types of unemployment which affect large numbers of workers, may be characterized as the "faces" of unemployment, each one requiring a different approach to solution.

The Three Faces of Unemployment

The American economy—today, more than ever, influenced by and interdependent on a world economy that is constantly in flux—is a complex weave of trends with both short- and long-term implications for workers, their communities and the nation as a whole. As an aspect of the overall economy, America's labor economy is ever characterized by both temporary and long-term unemployment, frequently recurring recessions followed by less-than-complete recoveries, and constant shifts in demand for skilled and semi-skilled labor. An examination of unemployment, as it results from this confluence of trends and activity, reveals three distinct types or manifestations of the problem:

■ Frictional Unemployment—defined as a joblessness resulting from the movement of workers from one employ to another or from hiatuses brought by career changes, childbearing, etc.

■ Cyclical Unemployment—determined by inevitable downturns (recessions) in the economy, regular downturns in certain industries and the effects of both on labor demand.

■ Structural Unemployment—joblessness, often long in duration, which emanates largely from deficiencies in workers' skills, disparities between workers' skills and in-demand skills, insufficiency of jobs and discrimination.

5

Of the three forms, the least problematic—both in numbers and complexity—is frictional unemployment. For many workers, this typically finite period of joblessness is elective; so too are the timing and points of re-entry into the active labor force. Given, however, the widespread phenomenon of the two-wage-earner family and the fact that individuals can anticipate multiple career changes in their working lifetimes, efforts to mitigate frictional unemployment should focus on promoting flexible work arrangements and career transitional assistance.

Cyclical unemployment, in the abstract, should resolve itself in the same way that economic "recoveries" resolve recessions. Were the world of work an abstraction and recessions less frequent and much shorter than history records, recoveries might well obviate concerns over the need for countercyclical employment programs, hiring incentives and enhanced social insurance benefits. The reality of cyclical unemployment is that recessions produce a "stair-step" effect on overall unemployment, an effect which serves to add numbers to the ranks of the long-term unemployed, thus contributing to the third and most pernicious form of unemployment—structural employment.

Multiple and complex in its dimensions, structural unemployment, in its broadest sense, represents the separation of workers from the means of economic self-sufficiency—a job. Often this separation is prolonged, in other cases, periodic and chronic; for some, the separation is likely to be permanent. What accounts for structural unemployment is not easily discernible; its roots are often a braid of personal, family, social and economic problems. That structural unemployment is most prevalent among the poor irrespective of color, ethnicity or region suggests

that one of these problems—economics—has an impact overwhelming all others.

Regarding the combined effects of circumstances surrounding the structurally unemployed, author Daniel Saks observed:

" . . . Not all members of (society) are born into the same situations, share the same experiences or are affected equally by their experience. Such differences generate special problems for some individuals because of discrimination, background, locations, occupations, or industry of employment."[3]

Considered together, the three faces of unemployment present formidable barriers to self-sufficiency, to family and community stability and, indeed, to the economic growth and human resource development of the entire nation. The actual numbers of Americans affected—in some instances victimized—by unemployment is a matter marked by discrepancies, disagreement and, in no small measure, politics. While there may be disputes as to its numbers, the one certain and irrefutable fact about unemployment in America, particularly its structural component, is that it is a growing problem, growing in complexity and inadequacy of solutions, as well as in numbers.

A Growing Problem

In the most general of terms, the growth of unemployment may be traced by charting increases in the rates of joblessness over a given period of time. (See Figure 1). In somewhat more focused terms, the increases in actual numbers of unemployed persons, especially among segments of the population most susceptible to joblessness, reveal growth in the dimensions of unemployment. With respect to both measures, however, there is dispute over precisely who should be counted as being unemployed, thus variations in both rates and numbers are advanced according to one's predilections.

Official Versus Real Unemployment

Are "official" unemployment figures, as reported by the federal goverment's Bureau of Labor Statistics and based on selected State Employment Service data, "real" in the sense that they accurately reflect the total numbers of people out of work? Or are "real" unemployment levels, as propounded by many non-government experts, accurate in their addition of the numbers of *underemployed*[4] and *discouraged*[5] workers to "official" figures? Given the philosophic and political overtones of both positions in this essentially method-

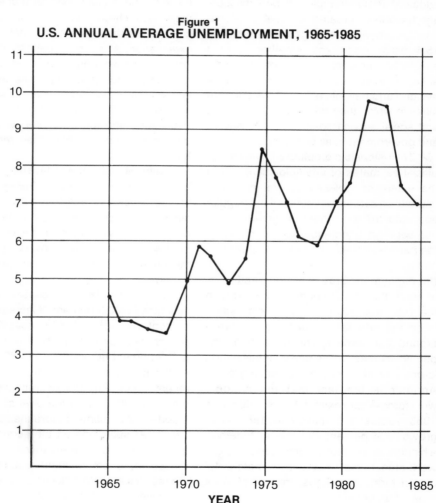

Figure 1
U.S. ANNUAL AVERAGE UNEMPLOYMENT, 1965-1985

DATA SOURCE: U.S. Department of Labor, Bureau of Labor Statistics

ological dispute, a definitive answer to either question is quite difficult to find. The discrepancy between official and real unemployment—regardless of one's subscription—is revealing nonetheless of the extent of joblessness among Americans. Whereas, for the year 1984, the nation's official unemployment rate was 7.5 percent—which represented 8.4 million of the total 112 million person labor force—the addition of underemployed and discouraged workers created a "real" national unemployment level of 13.6 percent, or 15.4 million Americans. Whether counted as officially unemployed or not, the presence of these "other" individuals has a decided and tangible effect on the communities in which they live and on the human and social service costs which taxpayers and government at all levels incur.

The ostensible problem with relying on official estimates of unemployment is that the extent of joblessness, its magnified impacts on certain segments of the population, and full awareness of growth in its numbers go underassessed, diminishing the perceived level of needed response.

Unemployment Growth in Perspective

In 1965, the official unemployment rate in the U.S. was 4.5 percent. Twenty years later the official national rate hovers around 7.0 percent. The more-than-fifty-percent increase in the rate over this period is one indication of the problem's growth. Another is the fact that the nation's workforce—approximately 74 million in 1965 versus 116 million in 1985—has grown by 36 percent. Considered together, a higher rate of unemployment and a larger workforce reveal that approximately 4.7 million more Americans are out of work today than in 1965.

What accounts for such an increase in the numbers of unemployed workers? For certain, the entrance of the 1946-64 baby boom generation into the labor force has swelled the ranks of workers seeking employment, thus intensifying competition for a limited number of jobs. Another contributor was the upsurge in inflation during the 1970s, brought on chiefly by increased energy costs which inhibited economic and, hence, employment growth.

Increases in structural unemployment, however, particularly long-term unemployment and chronic joblessness, are accounted for through a somewhat different explanation. A recurrent pattern of recessions in the economy, followed by less-than-full periods of recovery, has produced incremental increases in the numbers of workers who become unemployed during recessions and for whom recoveries are insufficient to bring about their reemployment.

In terming this the "Stairstep Pattern" of unemployment, the U.S. Bureau of Labor Statistics has noted that the result is higher levels of joblessness at the beginning of each succeeding recession. Tracing recent recessions/recovery cycles on the chart in Figure 2 demonstrates this pattern.

Before the 1969-70 recession, the jobless rate was 3.5 percent. It increased to 5 percent before the 1973-75 recession, to 6 percent before the 1980-81 downturn, and to 7.2 percent before the 1981-82 decline. At the height of recovery from this most recent recession, the overall unemployment rate returned to the level at which it stood—7.2 percent—before the recession began. At such time as the economy begins to move downward toward the next recession, unemployment will likely increase, once again reflecting a pre-recession level higher than the previous one.

In addition to the "creeping up" of threshold unemployment levels, there is

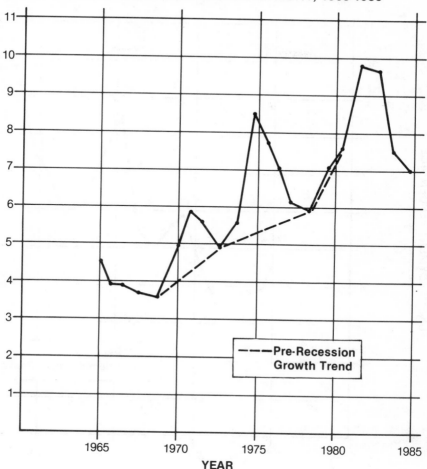

Figure 2
GROWTH IN PRE-RECESSION UNEMPLOYMENT, 1965-1985

UNEMPLOYMENT PERCENTAGE (seasonally adjusted)

YEAR

- - - - Pre-Recession Growth Trend

DATA SOURCE: U.S. Department of Labor, Bureau of Labor Statistics

also the problem of increasingly high levels of joblessness at the height of recessionary periods. Tracing these high points (see Figure 3) reveals that, with the exception of the 1980-81 recession, unemployment at the apex of each recession was higher than the apex of the previous one. For example, at the height of the 1981-82 recession, official unemployment reached 10.7 percent (11.4 percent unadjusted), representing in numbers more Americans out of work than at any time since the Great Depression. In many areas of the country, most notably cities, levels of unemployment were twice the national average, and even higher among selected segments of urban populations. As recessions continue to occur with an almost predictable regu-

9

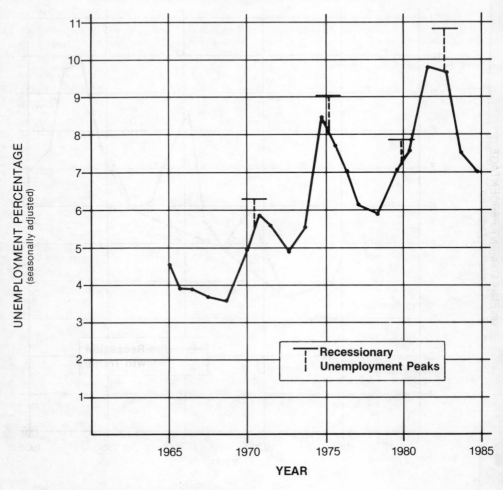

Figure 3
PEAK PERIODS OF UNEMPLOYMENT, 1965-1985

UNEMPLOYMENT PERCENTAGE
(seasonally adjusted)

YEAR

Recessionary
Unemployment Peaks

DATA SOURCE: U.S. Department of Labor, Bureau of Labor Statistics

larity, and as threshold unemployment levels increase with each recession, it is also quite likely that peak unemployment levels will continue to surpass previous highs.

From a public policy standpoint, incremental increases in unemployment, whatever the cause or explanation, have resulted in a gradual increase in the acceptable level of joblessness. "Accept-able" in this case represents the level above which efforts to reduce unemployment contribute to inflation, i.e., the Phillips curve. In determining what is an acceptable level of unemployment in relation to inflation, there are, however, inherent trade-offs to be made. For instance, it is estimated that, for every 1 percent of inflation saved by not reducing unemployment,

10

1 million jobs are lost in the economy. To the 8.4 million Americans "officially" unemployed or the 15.4 million "really" unemployed, such a trade-off would seem rather unfair, since inflation is quite relative when there are no earnings to spend.

Who Are The Unemployed?

With the exception of individuals transitioning between jobs (frictionally unemployed) and those in occupations which experience periodic downturns (cyclically unemployed), the majority of unemployed Americans have traditionally been youths and adults living in or close to poverty.

Their circumstance is captured in another observation by Saks: "Many disadvantaged adults were youth with labor market problems earlier and will be elderly workers in distress later."[6] The gloomy scenario described in this statement suggests that one's beginnings in poverty are likely to be perpetuated and, extending the thesis, passed on to one's future generations. The family histories of many Americans living in poverty unfortunately bear this out.

A July 1985 report of the Full Employment Action Council, a Washington-based coalition of organizations concerned with unemployment, found that 23 percent of unemployed Americans live below the poverty line, an increase of 9 percent over the last five years.[7] Among long-term unemployed persons—those out of work for more than twenty-six weeks—the poverty rate is 36 percent.

The relationship between poverty and unemployment is even more telling among specific segments of the population. For example, the FEAC report cited 61.6 percent of unemployed female heads of household as living in poverty, along with 51.7 percent of Blacks, 43.4 percent of Hispanics and 32.1 percent of Whites.

More recently, however, unemployment has extended its reach to a new segment of Americans, a segment characterized by long, stable work histories often with a single employer and often in well-paying occupations. "Dislocated" or "displaced" workers, as they are known, represent a quite different group of unemployed Americans, in that the roots of their joblessness have little in common with poverty, lack of skills or lack of experience. In the absence of solutions to their re-employment problems, however, dislocated workers find much in common with the unemployed poor and near poor.

A Special Problem for Youth

Of the more than 8 million Americans unemployed in 1985, nearly 38 percent are under the age of twenty-five. For youth overall, this means an unemployment rate of 17.3 percent.

For some subsets of the youth population, Black teenagers for instance, the unemployment numbers are much higher. While unemployment among White teenagers today stands at 15.1 percent, the rate for Black teens is more than twice that at 38.3 percent. Viewed another way, only 24.4 percent of Black and 38.1 percent of Hispanic teenagers are employed, while some 48.7 percent of White teenagers hold jobs. When the measurement is of full-time employment only, these percentages are even lower.

Despite a decline in the youth population of 11.5 percent between 1979 and 1984, the longer-term view of youth unemployment is equally dismal. During this same five-year period, the number of employed teenagers dropped by more than 20 percent. Participation by poor and minority youth dropped even more.

The statistics could go on. They reveal

a critical problem that is worsening. The causes of youth unemployment, while discernible, nonetheless seem to escape solution. The basic ones are summarized here.

Basic Skills
By far the most influential factor contributing to youth unemployment is lack of basic educational skills. The extent of these basic skills deficiencies was reflected in a 1976 nationwide study which found that 56 percent of Black youth and 44 percent of Hispanic youth were functionally illiterate, compared to only 13 percent of youth overall. Linked closely to the lack of basic skills among youth is the school dropout rate, in New York City, 70 percent among Blacks, 80 percent among Hispanics. In Chicago, the overall dropout rate is 45 percent, with 14,000 additional students joining the dropout ranks each year.

Lack of Jobs
The second major factor in high levels of unemployment for disadvantaged youth is a lack of jobs. Despite the strongest of economies, the number of jobs—particularly full-time jobs—for which disadvantaged youth can qualify is severely limited. The inadequacy of job supply is heightened in certain areas, such as older urban areas, rural areas and communities impacted by high unemployment, plant closings, etc. In these areas, competition between adults and youths for scarce job opportunities invariably places inexperienced youth workers at a disadvantage.

Other factors in the youth unemployment equation include: a lack of access to jobs, resulting from various forms of discrimination; a lack of knowledge of how to find and compete for openings in the job market; limited English-speaking abilities on the parts of ethnic minority youth; and, far from least in importance, the problem of teenage pregnancy, experienced by an estimated 20 percent of teenage women by age seventeen.

Hard-to-Employ Adults
Given the employment problems encountered by disadvantaged youth, it is hardly surprising that, unresolved, they continue to be problems when youths become adults. Deficiencies in reading and computational skills, lack of experience through lack of access to jobs, and discrimination in the workplace affect adult workers in much the same way they affect youth.

One major difference between youth and adult unemployment is the distribution of its impact within the latter group. Simply stated, unemployment has a greater impact on adult women, primarily because childbearing and single parenting create a special barrier to holding jobs. The fact that many disadvantaged women become mothers while still youths themselves explains the lack of educational and skill development from which many adult women suffer.

Other segments of the unemployed adult population include long-term unemployed and discouraged persons—many of whom have some form of handicap, addiction or history of involvement with the law—and minority group members in greater proportions than their proportion to the overall population. While the numbers of unemployed adults vary according to definition and methodology for counting, a good approximation is about 7 million. Most, if not all, of this group suffer from unemployment that is structural in nature.

The problems of unemployed adult workers are, in some ways, more complex and difficult to ameliorate than problems affecting youth, again particularly for women with children. Since many adults were themselves school dropouts as youths, illiteracy and basic skill deficiencies inhibit their chances of obtaining decent jobs. Yet getting adults into remedial and basic educational programs is often extremely difficult, owing in large part to the length of time away from school and, for single heads of household, commitments to children. In addition, the reluctance of employers to hire adults with poorly developed work histories creates a problem of access to jobs for unemployed adults.

Dislocated Workers

The third major segment of unemployed Americans, dislocated workers, presents a set of circumstances and problems quite different from those of disadvantaged youths or adults. On one hand, the profile of the dislocated worker, with typically long and stable work and earnings histories, highly developed skills, good work habits, etc., suggests many advantages over the other two groups. On the other hand, older age, sometimes obsolete skills, lack of basic education and high expectations of future earnings can frequently inhibit the dislocated workers' chances of successfully transitioning into new employment. Other difficulties are presented by the fact that many dislocated workers are long-time residents of the communities in which they live, have deep family ties and often own property, all circumstances which mitigate against moving to areas where new opportunities might exist.

The roots of the dislocated worker problem typically lie in macroeconomic trends and changes which influence microeconomic decisions. Stated another way, shifts in the national and international economies tend to determine whether industries grow or decline, hence whether factories and stores expand or close their doors. In some cases, the circumstances surrounding a business closing are particular to that business, e.g., bankruptcy, catastrophe, retirement or death of the owner, etc., but the major causes of dislocation have more to do with the structure of the economy. In a somewhat different sense than hard-to-employ adults, dislocated workers too are victims of structural unemployment.

As in the case of disadvantaged adults, discrepancies and uncertainties exist over the precise number of dislocated workers. This is particularly the case when estimates are made during periods of recession, when layoffs and unemployment may be cyclical (temporary) as opposed to structural (permanent). Current estimates range from as low as 100,000 to over 3 million, depending on the criteria used to count.

Regardless of the estimate chosen however, there is little dispute over the point that dislocated workers—defined as out of work with little or no chance of being recalled or reemployed within the same industry—are a growing phenomenon. The Bureau of Labor Statistics estimates that 11.5 million jobs were lost in the economy between 1979 and 1984 alone. Current trends in the economy and in the behavior of many industries and corporations suggest that dislocation will continue.

Addressing the problems of dislocated workers involves sensitive issues of age, educational deficiencies, retraining, and changes in income. In addition, the personal problems of adjustment and self-esteem must be dealt with in shaping alternatives.

Unemployment in Cities

At the beginning of this chapter, it was suggested that urban unemployment problems differ from non-urban problems not in type, but rather in magnitude. Having defined the types of unemployment common to both, it remains to suggest how they differ in magnitude.

Unemployment Rates

A survey of 388 U.S. cities, conducted in mid-1984 by the National League of Cities (NLC), sought to identify, among other things, the levels of joblessness in urban communities. Among its findings was that 45 percent of the cities surveyed had unemployment rates of 8 percent or more at a time when the national rate—at the height of the economy's recovery—approached 7 percent. In sharper contrast to the national average, 22 percent of the cities reported unemployment rates of over 10 percent. In central cities, where population densities are highest, 57 percent reported jobless rates of over 10 percent. Among the cities in this category were: Buffalo, Birmingham, Ala., Cleveland, Detroit, Eugene, Ore., Gary and Hartford. The regional distribution of these cities suggests that high unemployment is not a "frostbelt" versus "sunbelt" phenomenon, but rather a problem which dramatically affects certain segments of the population wherever they live.

More telling than the comparison of city and national unemployment rates is a look at unemployment as it affects certain segments of urban populations. In Detroit, for example, the level of joblessness among Black teenagers in some neighborhoods exceeds 60 percent. This level is nearly double the national average for Black teenagers, itself a deplorably high 38.3 percent. The circumstances of Black youth in the inner-city neighborhoods of many other U.S. cities are quite similar. Offering a general observation on the problem, Freeman and Holzer wrote in *The Public Interest* earlier this year: "In short, the more narrowly one focuses on inner-city youth in poverty neighborhoods, the worse the problem looks.[8]

Unemployment Among Cities

Unemployment, overall, is a high priority for cities of all sizes. Sixty-two percent of cities in the NLC survey identified unemployment as the top or a high priority among problems in their communities. A nearly equal percentage see unemployment retaining this priority for the forseeable future.

Distinctions in unemployment problems among U.S. cities exist primarily in the degrees and priorities of specific problems in each community. The NLC survey, for instance, found that cities with the highest unemployment rates (over 10 percent) ranked "job creation" as their highest priority for action, while cities with low unemployment cited the "lack of basic and specialized skills among youth and adults" as their highest priority.

A second set of distinctions relates, in general, to differences in city sizes. One example of this distinction is that almost twice as many small cities view the need for more jobs as their top priority than do large cities. Another is that problems related to the educational and skill deficiencies of youth represent severe problems for 82 percent of large cities, but for only 38 percent of those with under 50,000 populations. A similar distinction exists with respect to the severity of adult skills deficiencies.

Among regions of the country, distinctions in the priorities of cities tend to occur along job creation versus skill training lines. Cities in the Northcentral and Southern regions prioritized the need for job creation, while their counterparts in the Northeast and West see the need for skill training among youth and adults as most important. Here too, the "frostbelt" versus "sunbelt" stereotypes do not stand up.

With respect to priorities for serving problem segments of the urban populations, there is less distinction among cities over the top priority. Groups receiving the top priority ranking most often were: high school dropouts (22 percent), dislocated workers (19 percent), youth in school (17 percent) and welfare recipients (12 percent). This relative evenness among the top-ranked groups suggests, perhaps, that the problems of each are viewed as very high priorities in all cities.

What can be said about distinctions in unemployment problems among cities is that they exist within broad commonalities of problems, populations and needs. To the extent that this is true, the discussion and examples to follow of what works to reduce unemployment in cities will also have commonalities among cities.

Beyond the Numbers

The relationship of joblessness to other social and human resource problems suggests a broader context for viewing the magnitude of unemployment in cities. Poverty, crime, homelessness, poor health and nutrition, family break-up and social unrest are all contributors to and outgrowths of unemployment problems. As they intermix in cities and touch large numbers of people living in close proximity to one another, their magnitudinal impact is indeed greater than it is outside of cities.

This interrelation of unemployment and other social problems also offers a plausible explanation of why nearly two-thirds of local officials responding in the NLC survey cited unemployment as the top or a high priority in their community.

That nearly an equal percentage of these officials see unemployment remaining the top or a high priority in the forseeable future is evidence of the problem's entrenchment.

The difficulty in dealing with a problem such as unemployment in cities is that competition for limited resources ultimately dilutes the level of effort required. The consequence of diluted efforts to ameliorate unemployment, as with other problems, is that rather than improve, the problem typically worsens. A comparative assessment of the unemployment problem of, for example, inner-city minority youths today and twenty years ago would reveal a measurable worsening of the problem. Coincident or not, the accompanying fact is that proportionately less federal assistance is today available to combat unemployment than in the past.

Beyond the issue of resources with which to address unemployment in cities, a larger problem emanates from trends within the national as well as the world economy. In the four decades since the end of World War II, American cities have witnessed a steady outmigration of industry and, with it, jobs. Several factors account for this migratory trend, which first carried jobs to the suburbs, later to different regions of the country, and, more recently, offshore or overseas.

Irrespective of the economic explanation of this trend, the fact remains that jobs which once provided a start for unskilled and undereducated workers are today becoming increasingly scare. And nowhere is the magnitude of consequent unemployment and related problems greater than in America's cities.

FOOTNOTES

[1] The 1985 Statistical Abstract of the United States, U.S. Department of Commerce, Bureau of the Census.

[2] U.S. Department of Labor, Bureau of Labor Statistics, 1985.

[3] Saks, Daniel, Distressed Workers in the Eighties (Washington, D.C., National Planning Association, 1983), p.5.

[4] "Underemployment" refers to workers who, involuntarily, are forced to work in part-time jobs with typically low wages, poor benefits and no upward mobility.

[5] "Discouraged" workers are individuals with the desire to hold jobs who, for various reasons, have given up seeking employment.

[6] Saks, op. cit. p. vii.

[7] "First Friday Report", Full Employment Action Council, Washington, D.C., July 5, 1985.

[8] Freeman, Richard B. and Holzer, Harry J. "Young Blacks and Jobs-What We Now Know," The Public Interest, No. 78, Winter, 1985, p. 21.

Chapter 2

REDUCING URBAN UNEMPLOYMENT
What Works At the Local Level

REDUCING URBAN UNEMPLOYMENT
What Works at the Local Level

In the following three chapters, a series of twenty-one initiatives aimed at reducing unemployment in cities is presented. Targeted to specific aspects of unemployment, these initiatives are categorized according to the three segments of urban populations most impacted by the problem: disadvantaged youth, hard-to-employ adults and dislocated workers. The term "initiative" is used here to encompass the breadth and variety of local efforts to address unemployment and related human and social problems.

Indeed, the twenty-one initiatives presented in this book reflect a variety of program approaches, strategies and partnerships, the origins of which are equally varied. What is shared by all twenty-one is an overriding concern for a problem within the community and the determination to address it with every resource available. That they are local initiatives, albeit involving resources and expertise from outside the community as well as within, is the other characteristic common to all.

Considerations in Selection

The criteria for selection of local initiatives were developed with the basic purpose of this book in mind—to provide examples of successful local efforts for the consideration of communities in search of new or better approaches to unemployment and related problems. The first consideration, then, was replicability. Would elements and contributing factors have sufficiently common strains to be adaptable, in whole or in part, in other cities?

The second criterion had to do with commonality in the definition and dimensions of the problem ("problem" here defined as an aspect of the broader youth, adult or dislocated worker problem). Does this condition reflect similar conditions in other communities?

A third criterion resulted from an interest in representing a cross-section of America's cities, in terms of size, region, demographics, etc. In this instance, the criterion applied more to selection within each of the three group-categories.

The fourth criterion, though not last in importance or weight, referred to the lessons which various local initiatives offered. By "lesson" is meant the value of the experience in addressing a particular aspect of unemployment. While results, in terms of numbers trained or placed or jobs created, were a certain consideration in the selection process, care was exercised not to overemphasize quantifiable aspects when the quality of approach (e.g., appropriate linkages, combinations of resources, etc.) may well be more instructive for replication. This qualified interpretation of the success of initiatives acknowledges, in part, the dimensions of urban unemployment being such that "solution" is most often a misnomer and that "reduction" is the more realistic goal.

Within the "Disadvantaged Youth," "Hard-to-Employ Adults" and "Dislocated Workers" categories, additional criteria were employed in the selection and ordering of cases. Selections were made in the interest of presenting as many aspects of the broader problem in each category as possible. A brief description of each case appears in the introductions to Chapters 3, 4 and 5.

General Observations on What Works

Individually, the twenty-one case studies offer insights into the needs and problems of urban America's most disadvantaged groups. More importantly, they suggest approaches to those needs and problems which, in some measure, have worked in the communities from which the studies have been drawn. As such, the cases represent models of local-level programs, strategies, linkages or "initiatives" for other communities to consider.

Beyond their individual contributions to reducing unemployment among various groups of urban residents, the case studies collectively offer insights into what works at the local level. These conceptual lessons on what contributes to the success of local efforts, as they derive from cities of all types, sizes and regions of the country, are instructive not only of employment-related initiatives, but of other types as well. In addition to their lessons, the case studies collectively present a composite view of the human resource dilemma confronting urban America today.

On Different Needs and Different Solutions

When I described to a colleague the division of case studies into categories of "Disadvantaged Youth," "Hard-to-Employ Adults" and "Dislocated Workers," his reply was to say that urban unemployment was, then, not a single problem, but rather several different problems. The observation was quite astute. Hence, while commonalities exist among the contributing factors to each group's problems, i.e., insufficient numbers of jobs, skill deficiencies, etc., specificity is needed in the definition of each problem as the first step toward solution.

At the heart of virtually all employment and related problems are needs: for education, basic or remedial; for skills training or retraining; for experience; or for knowledge of how to find a job. That these needs differ among youth, adults and dislocated workers is readily observable. The needs of New York and Chicago's inner-city youth, for example, are quite different from those of San Francisco's homeless adults or Des Moines' dislocated factory workers and farmers. So too are the needs of Yakima Valley, Washington's small-town youth different from those of Baltimore's AFDC recipients or the laid-off copper miners of Butte-Silver Bow, Montana.

That needs differ also within subsets of each group is, on the surface, less readily observable. For this reason, the selections of local initiatives in each of the three categories were based, in part, on an interest in presenting a cross-section of each group's problems.

Within the Disadvantaged Youth category, for example, the specific needs of Albuquerque's pregnant and parenting teenagers differ from those of Sacramento's Local Conservation Corps participants, and, alternatively, San Jose's predominantly Hispanic youth population has different needs from those of New Bedford and Cape Cod's primarily White and English-speaking youth. Within a given community, as Minneapolis' trio of youth programs reflect, needs differ even among segments of the youth population, thus necessitating different approaches to each.

Similar differences exist within the Hard-to-Employ Adults group. Here, for example, the differences between San Antonio's unskilled adult workers, whose needs for English language and basic skills are great, and Minneapolis' long-term unemployed adults, 78 percent of whom are high school graduates, are quite clear. Another example is the contrasting needs of Baltimore and Denver's female-dominated AFDC populations and the largely male composition of San Francisco's homeless community.

Among dislocated workers, the distinctions in needs derive primarily from the circumstances which bring about displacement. Examples of differences are Buffalo and Erie County, where the general decline of the area's economy has created a dispersed dislocated worker population, and Fort Wayne, where a specific plant closing brought about problems for an occupationally-similar group of workers. Further distinctions exist between regions of the country, as evidenced by needs of Eugene and Springfield, Oregon's dislocated timber industry workers versus Metropolitan St.Louis' chiefly manufacturing workers.

The point in emphasizing differences in needs—among groups as well as within each group—is to suggest two keys to success in addressing them. The first key is targeting of efforts and resources to a specific segment of the population in need. Accurate targeting requires a clear identification of the need (or needs), including type of need, scope of the need and size of the population. Each of the twenty-one initiatives in the following chapters, in varying ways and degrees, is targeted to a specific need.

The second key to successfully addressing needs is tailoring of programs, strategies, etc., to meet the identified need. Tailored approaches involve the application of resources and services in ways in which the population can identify with and make use of them to create solutions for themselves. Tailoring is also a characteristic feature of all twenty-one initiatives, examples being Minneapolis' trio of youth programs, Tampa's municipal employment program and Butte-Silver Bow's customized training programs.

On Different Sources Of Initiative

The term "initiative" is used throughout this book to refer to a broad range of local efforts to reduce unemployment. In a somewhat different sense here, it refers to the action taken by an individual(s) or group(s) to set an effort in motion. In the twenty-one cases, the initiative in responding to an identified need or problem comes from a variety of sources within the community. What they have in common is a deep concern for the persons in need and an equally deep interest in addressing the situation.

Local elected officials (LEO's), by the nature of their office, have a vested concern for the needs of the unemployed in their communities. What determines the level of response by LEO's most often has to do with the personal and political priorities of the individual official, his or her expertise and creativity in the matter, the competency of city departments, and competing community problems.

In nine of the twenty-one cases, local elected officials are the initiators—the primary movers—behind their respective community's effort. Each case reflects different types of cities, different natures of problems and different circumstances surrounding them. The nine cases are: Minneapolis' youth programs, San Antonio's job creation effort, Baltimore and Denver's "welfare-to-work" programs, Portland's "first source" hiring approach, San Francisco's homeless persons projects, Des Moines' dislocated worker center and Butte-Silver Bow's retraining programs. Most instructive about the role of local elected officials is the unique opportunity it presents to marshall community resources, focus community attention and coordinate the efforts of other contributors to a local effort. The results of these nine LEO-initiated efforts, as the case studies describe, attest to the potential contribution local officials can make to unemployment-reducing efforts.

Private industry, otherwise referred to as the business community, has always had significant potential for contributing to local employment efforts. Typically limiting the actual role of the private sector has been a lack of understanding on the parts of both public and private leadership of what role employers can play. With the passage of the Job Training Partnership Act (JTPA) in 1982, a legally-mandated role in employment and training for the private sector was established through Private Industry Councils (PICs). In addition to setting priorities among local employment and training needs, the PICs have a determining role in the funding of local JTPA programs for youth, adults and dislocated workers. (See discussion of resources below)

In six of the cases, the private sector took the initiative to sponsor or develop an effort to reduce local unemployment. Four of the five cases are to be found in the Dislocated Worker Chapter (5), which is not surprising given the connection to dislocation which is shared by both business and workers. Three of the dislocated worker initiatives spearheaded by the private sector, Buffalo and Erie County, Metropolitan St. Louis and Eugene/Springfield, are today operated by or through PICs. The fourth private sector initiative on behalf of dislocated workers was a company-specific effort, undertaken in conjunction with organized labor in Fort Wayne.

Two private sector efforts on behalf of disadvantaged youth, one of them a PIC initiative in New Bedford and Cape Cod, the other a Small Business Administration

effort in Sacramento, appear in Chapter 3. The New Bedford and Cape Cod CCP Learning Centers is a rather novel PIC initiative, in that it is directly tied into the public school systems. Sacramento's SBA effort to create a local conservation corps for youth originated as a summer experiment based on California's successful statewide program and became a year-round program one year later.

As a source of leadership or participation in local employment/unemployment efforts, the private sector—in particular, the Private Industry Councils—has much to contribute in the way of resources, tailoring of programs and training curricula and sources of jobs. In nearly all of the cases, the relationship of individual employers is also critical to the bottom-line success of efforts to reduce unemployment—jobs.

Community based organizations (CBOs), as their generic name implies, are integrally tied to the lives of community residents and, hence, to their problems. Frequently, CBOs emerge as a grassroots response to problems which seem to escape solution through other means. While some CBOs exist to serve limited community needs or functions, many are multiple-service centers which address all types of human needs.

Of the twenty-one initiatives, CBOs are responsible for five. While differing in type, each shares origins within its respective community. Yakima Valley and, originally, San Jose's youth programs were initiated as local OIC (Occupational Industrialization Center) programs. Albuquerque's New Futures School began out of the basement of the local YWCA. New York City's dropout prevention and assistance effort, Operation Success, is the brainchild of the nonprofit Federation Employment and Guidance Service, and Chicago's Alternative

Schools Network numbers fifty CBO's working on behalf of that city's school dropouts.

The role of foundations or philanthropies in community initiatives is most often one of contributing resources. In Minneapolis, not only did a local foundation, the McKnight Foundation, provide resources for a combination of programs to employ that city's long-term unemployed, it initiated the effort by soliciting proposals from both Minneapolis' and St. Paul's mayors. The result of the Foundation's initiative, aside from the jobs it produced, was the eventual enactment of a statewide program based on the local model.

On Resources, Partnerships and Sharing
Critical to the success of the local initiatives profiled in this book are creative, innovative and effective uses of resources. In twenty of the twenty-one cases—Denver's STEPS Program is the exception—resources are derived from more than a single source, and, in most cases, from several sources. The combinations of resources, in addition to enlarging a resource base, typically reflect a partnership effort in the planning, design and implementation of local initiatives. Ultimately, as the cases will evidence, this sharing of resources and effort contributes to broader and more effective services to people in need.

The one resource common to the twenty multi-resource efforts is the Job Training Partnership Act (JTPA). The presence of JTPA resources in all but one initiative suggests its importance as a key ingredient in successful programming. Uses of JTPA Title II-A and II-B funds for disadvantaged youth programs, Title II-A funds for adult programs, and Title III funds for dislocated worker programs offer broad possibilities for effective responses to local needs. Used in combination with other funds from typically less restrictive sources, JTPA resources provide a solid base for basic and remedial education programs, skills training and retraining and some supportive services. The case studies also reveal effective uses of JTPA funds for leveraging funds from other sources.

In addition to JTPA, a host of local government, state government, private industry and foundation funds are utilized in the programs and services detailed in the cases. Descriptions of the ways in which these funds are procured, the relationships between multiple funding sources, and their impacts on the quality and scale of local efforts will be left to the case studies themselves. It is worth noting here, however, that the lone initiative funded from a single source—while sound in its programmatic model—nevertheless ended after two successful years when the sole source of support ended.

Other Observations
Beyond their examples of targeting, tailoring, leadership initiative, partnerships and resourceful financing, the case studies provide the interested reader with a sense of the "intangibles" that contribute to, if not determine, the success of local efforts to reduce unemployment. These elements include: sensitivity and concern for the needs of persons in disadvantaged circumstances, commitment to high-quality efforts in response to those needs, and dedication to achieving results.

In sum, this combination of tangible and intangible features incorporated in the following case studies suggests that local efforts to reduce urban unemployment can and do work effectively.

Using the Case Studies

Our purpose in presenting information on reducing urban unemployment in the form of case studies is to provide other communities with the fullest sense possible of the circumstances, problems and factors surrounding the evolution and development of successful local initiatives. Important to note is what works well in one community may not work the same way in another. On the other hand, it is perhaps quite likely that certain elements, components, features, etc., of the initiatives profiled here may well merit incorporation, in some form or dimension, into a community's existing efforts.

The information presented in the case studies is done so in summary form. The inclusion of a contact person at the end of each study is intended for use in learning more about the experience of that community. It is our hope that readers will make use of these contacts in their own pursuits of successful initiatives to reduce urban unemployment.

Chapter 3

DISADVANTAGED YOUTH
Overcoming Barriers to Employment

DISADVANTAGED YOUTH
Overcoming Barriers to
Employment

America's disadvantaged youth population faces multiple barriers to a successful entry into the world of work. This is particularly true of the large numbers of youth who live in poverty-stricken neighborhoods of the nation's cities. Failing to overcome these barriers as youth virtually assures that they will continue during adulthood, with serious implications for employment, earnings and susceptibility to social problems.

More than any other factor, deficiencies in basic education skills prevent the successful assimilation of disadvantaged youth into the labor market. For this reason, all eight case studies of disadvantaged youth initiatives incorporate some element of basic or remedial education into their program structure, while distinct in their overall design and their objectives. The cases also present distinct approaches to the issues of job creation and access to jobs for youth, as well as in the targeting of special needs within the disadvantaged youth population.

The first case, taken from the New Bedford and Cape Cod communities of southeastern Massachusetts, focuses on the use of state-of-the-art Comprehensive Competencies Programs (CCP's) to instruct students in basic skills. Established by the Private Industry Council, three CCP learning Centers, two operating in schools and one out of the PIC office, also combine world-of-work courses and occupational internships in a split day of academic and occupational training. Plans for year-round learning and development are being pursued through adaptation of summer youth employment programs.

Minneapolis, Minnesota is the source of the second study. In this community, three programs (a fourth is being developed) offer different approaches to different aspects of the disadvantaged youth problem. A school-to-work transition program using private sector internships for training, a summer youth employment program which ties work eligibility to the passage of academic benchmarks and a year-round program aimed at dropouts comprise the three. The programs are coordinated through the active leadership of Minneapolis' mayor and are supported by a local foundation.

A program to prevent students from dropping out of New York City's public schools is the focus of the third case study. An in-school approach to the problem, Operation Success provides comprehensive services to potential dropouts, including career development, vocational training and placement. In 1985, the program was operated in eleven of New York's high schools.

In Chicago, Illinois, a network of fifty "alternative schools" operated by community-based organizations address that city's school dropout populations. All but four of the schools offer programs leading to a high school diploma or Graduate Equivalent Degree (GED), and nearly half utilize comprehensive competency programs. Linkages with the Chicago PIC and the Mayor's Office of Employment and Training provide training and placement support as a complement to remedial instruction.

The fifth case study in this category describes Sacramento, California's Local Conservation Corps, an urban spinoff of the California Conservation Corps. Combining work experience and mandatory education and training, the Corps provides Sacramento poor and ethnic minority youth with valuable preparation for employment in a community service setting. The SLCC has received both praise and visibility in its first year of operations.

In Yakima, Washington, a fourteen-year-old Opportunities Industrialization Center (OIC) is the focal point for skills training, education, job placement and supportive services in a two-county area made up of small communities. The OIC operates from training centers and a satellite office, as well as a year-round educational clinic and an alternative high school, serving both migrants and year-round residents.

A national model for serving pregnant adolescents and adolescent parents is the subject of the seventh case. The New Futures School in Albuquerque, New Mexico, dates back to 1970 and has served nearly 4,000 clients, the majority of whom have been teenage mothers. Health, education and employment and training programs, with assistance from Albuquerque volunteers, make the school a tremendous resource for the city's adolescent women.

The final case study of Chapter 3 recounts the "barrio" origins of the Center for Employment Training (CET) in San Jose, California. Originally an OIC center, CET has been at the forefront of employment and training for San Jose's Hispanic community. Academic instruction, English-as-a-Second-Language, and counseling are also components of the Center's services.

INNOVATIVE APPROACHES TO REMEDIATION AND TRAINING

THE CCP LEARNING CENTERS
New Bedford and Cape Cod, Massachusetts

Of the many obstacles to youth entering employment, perhaps most pervasive and disabling of all is the lack of basic and functional skills. A delineation of "basic" (math, reading, language, science and social studies) and "functional" (occupational knowledge, consumerism, citizenship and life skills) deficiencies suggests that effective approaches to remediation require resources and expertise outside of traditional educational systems. Schools, however, remain the locus of activity, academic and non-academic, for the largest numbers of youth; thus, the challenge to communities is to link educational and non-educational resources (i.e., vocational training, summer youth employment, etc.) in such a way as to promote a successful transition from school to work.

In Southeastern Massachusetts, a partnership of employment and training and educational professionals has resulted in the enhancement of both basic and functional skills for three out of every four youth who enroll in the area's five "Learning Centers." Utilizing state-of-the-art Comprehensive Competencies Programs, the Centers—three of which have been established in high schools and two in local Private Industry Council (PIC) offices—combine a self-paced, computer-assisted instructional system with teacher-instructed classes in basic academic skills. With the involvement of private industry, the Learning Centers' curricula also includes world-of-work courses and occupational internships, with the student's day divided between academic study and occupational training. Efforts to create a year-round learning and development environment are being undertaken with the adaptation of summer youth employment programs to include academic instruction as well as on-the-job experience.

Background

The genesis of the CCP Learning Centers is rather unique, in that—despite its fundamentally educational nature—the idea for the centers originated with the Private Industry Council of the New Bedford JTPA Service Delivery Area. (The New Bedford SDA covers much of Southeastern Massachusetts, including Cape Cod.) Convinced that the Comprehensive Competencies Program approach offered significant potential for enhancing traditional education curricula and improving the school-to-work transitions, the PIC, through its administrative entity, the Office of Job Partnerships (OJP), initiated discussions with area school officials beginning in the fall of 1983. Equally convinced that incorporation of the CCP concept by school systems would require demonstrations of its effectiveness, feasibility and replicability, the OJP established CCP Learning Centers in its New Bedford and Hyannis offices in May and June 1984, respectively. Subsequently, proposals, in response to RFPs issued by the PIC, came from three schools within the area, two of which submitted a joint proposal.

Organizational Involvement and Funding

As a PIC initiative, the CCP Learning Centers project is funded and managed by the SDA administrative entity, the Office of Job Partnerships. In the cases of the three schools which have established Learning Centers—one is a local high school, another a regional high school and the third a regional technical high school—the involvement of school officials includes administrators, guidance counselors and teachers. The two centers operated out of PIC offices are run by staff hired by the OJP. Involvement of business, aside from the PIC itself, comes in the form of participation in development of the world-of-work curricula and in hiring relationships for occupational internships and summer positions (more on this below).

Funding arrangements for CCP Learning Centers reflect correspondingly the partnership which, from the outset, this initiative has represented. To capitalize and cover start-up costs for the Centers—estimated to be $50,000 per Center—JTPA monies from the Governor's Discretionary Fund (known generally as the "Eight Percent Set Aside" for educational coordination) were allocated in the amount of $442,000. Ongoing operation of the five centers is funded with $140,000 in JTPA Title II-A funds and in-kind contributions from each participating school of $1.50 for every $1.00 of funds provided by the OJP. In addition, the adapted versions of the Summer Youth Employment Program are funded through a $1.2 million SYEP allocation.

Characteristics of the Target Population

While much of New Bedford's JTPA Service Delivery Area is non-urban and, consequently, atypical of urban populations in most demographic respects, the economically disadvantaged status of CCP Learning Center participants is a shared characteristic. (Under JTPA requirements, at least 90 percent of service recipients must be economically disadvantaged; non-disadvantaged participants in the CCP Learning Centers are served with non-JTPA matching funds.) Characteristics of the New Bedford and Hyannis Centers participants include:

	New Bedford	Hyannis
Age		
14-17	17%	13%
18-21	24%	18%
22-24	51%	59%
55 and over	8%	10%
Sex		
male	30%	25%
female	70%	75%
Race		
White	64%	85%
Black	28%	9%
Hispanic	7%	2%
other	1%	4%
Education at entry		
Average grade level completed	10th	11th
Average reading level	9th	9th
Average math level	7th	7th

Key Elements

The Comprehensive Competencies Program

The concept of a Comprehensive Competencies Program is one of individualized and self-paced learning facilitated by the assistance of computers. Combined with instructor-taught courses in basic academic skills, the CCP concept enables flexibility in addressing individual learning needs as well as opportunities for individual exploration of career paths and occupational training. The diagnostic and prescriptive testing mechanisms built in to the computer-based system provide both rapid feedback and motivational incentives for the student to learn, as well as dramatic reductions in teacher time spent on curriculum planning, testing and guiding. In fact, as students and instructors become more familiar with the CCP format, it is possible for students to run the system themselves, thus freeing teachers' time to provide one-to-one instruction and problem-solving assistance.

The CCP model combines written, computerized and audiovisual materials to provide a diverse and inclusive curriculum, one which offers more in the way of instruction than most other systems currently used in remediation and training. Units of instruction are divided into lessons which are "bite size chunks" of material geared to specific learning objectives. The lessons include feedback to students which allows a sense of what has been accomplished. Expectations, based on the experience of using the CCP model, are for students to advance 1.5 to 2.0 grade levels for every one hundred hours of academic instruction in math, reading or language competency areas.

Integration of CCP's Into Traditional Educational Curricula

Among the three high schools into which the CCP Learning Centers have been incorporated, there has been variation in the ways and degrees to which the concept has been used. In all three, however, the Centers have become the hub around which assessment, diagnosis and coordination of academic and functional skills training revolve.

Variations among the schools include Cape Cod's Technical High's integration of the CCP into its career assessment and guidance program, a process which led to the establishment of a Career Development Center, as well as an evening offering of CCP instruction. In the jointly-operated programs of the Warehan and Old Rochester Regional High Schools, the CCP has been incorporated into overall academic curricula and is offered as a voluntary elective; a related world-of-work curricula addressing the sociology, psychology and economics of work was introduced in September 1985.

The Learning Centers operated out of the New Bedford and Hyannis PIC offices offer morning and afternoon CCP instruction, with evening and weekend offerings under consideration. Participating students in these two communities are referred to the Centers by the local high school.

Linking CCPs and Employment

In efforts to link basic and functional skill attainment with actual working experience, New Bedford JTPA officials have developed various approaches and are experimenting with others. One approach has been to incorporate world-of-work curricula, designed in collaboration with area employers, into all five Learning Centers as a pre-employment development tool. A second approach, involving private sector internships in which students spend 1/2 to 2/3 of their day, receive academic credit and, in some cases, pay, has focused on providing a variety of work experiences. Among the occupations for which internships have been developed are data entry, travel, insurance, banking and retail business, as well as hospital, library and law enforcement services. Where possible, student internships are continued as summer employment, reflecting the interest of both employment and training and educational professionals in a year-round approach to youth development.

To facilitate this year-round connection between CCP instruction and employment, the Office of Job Partnerships, during the summer of 1985, implemented three variation of its traditional Summer Youth Employment Program based on experimentation the summer before. The first variations, called the Vocational Explanation Program, involved the extension of the internships concept to summertime employment, in this case a rotation of three internships each lasting three weeks. Each of the 500 youth involved in the program was paid $3.75 per hour for a twenty-five-hour work week, with an additional five non-paid hours per week required for participation in structured learning and training. Academic benchmarks were developed by PIC staff and employers, with each business being asked to pledge $10.00 per week per student as a bonus incentive for meeting the benchmarks. The bonus money, distributed by the PIC, is tax-deductible for employers since the PIC is a nonprofit entity.

The second summer program, entitled Enriched Work Experiences and designed to serve 400-500 youths, provided up to twenty-four hours of work per week—at $3.50 per hour—in a variety of special projects in schools and other public facilities. Participants in these projects were also required to invest five non-paid hours per week in classroom education or job-related training. In some instances, academic credit was awarded for the time spent in training.

The third New Bedford summer employment initiative was the traditional summer youth experience program in which 200 youth worked twenty hours a week at the minimum wage ($3.35 per hour). Under this program, no academic requirement was involved, and no credit for work was awarded.

As an additional learning aid, the New Bedford PIC funded the purchase of a van, the mobile mission of which was to provide one-day work orientations at youth job sites.

Results

During the first summer—1984—in which the Comprehensive Competencies Program operated in the New Bedford Learning Centers, 75 percent of the youths who entered the four- to six-week program one to two grade levels behind came up to their own grade level. While evaluations of the CCP results for the 1984-85 school year have yet to be reported, New Bedford officials see indications of success similar to those of the summer programs.

Evaluations of the three 1985 summer employment programs which served youths were premature at this writing. The concept, however, of a year-round linkage between basic skills instruction and work experience training offers only positive expectations for the development of economically disadvantaged youth. As more and more educators and employment and training professionals call for year round schooling, instruction in the New Bedford

CCP Learning Centers may offer a more palatable, economic and, quite possibly, more effective youth development model.

For More Information, Contact:

Paul Vigeant, President or
Sylvia Beville, Special Projects Manager
Office of Job Partnerships
181 Hillman Street
New Bedford, MA 02140
(617) 999-3161

DIFFERENT STRATEGIES FOR DIFFERING NEEDS
A Trio of Programs for
Disadvantaged Youth

THE YOUTH WORK INTERNSHIP PROGRAM, THE SUMMER YOUTH EMPLOYMENT PROGRAM AND THE YEAR-ROUND YOUTH PROGRAM
Minneapolis, Minnesota

Sensitivity to different needs among disadvantaged youth. . . . *Concern* over how best to address different types of need. . . . And *commitment* on the parts of public, private and community leaders to do what it takes to see that needs are met. In local efforts to address the employment and related problems of disadvantaged youth, each of these represents an ingredient critical to success.

In the city of Minneapolis, sensitivity to the differing needs of in-school youths versus dropouts, academically deficient students versus unmotivated ones and younger versus older youths has led to the recognition that no one approach will work for all. A common concern among government and education officials, the private sector and community leaders, in turn, has led to the development of three discrete programs to address these differing needs. The commitment of all segments of the Minneapolis community together with leadership of the city's Mayor has resulted in the success of all three.

Background

The Youth Internship Program
Initiated by Mayor Don Fraser in 1983 out of concern for keeping Minneapolis' young people in school, the Youth Internship Program involved educational officials, the Chamber of Commerce and City Hall. In its first year the Program was implemented in three of the city's high schools, with 86 junior class members participating. Funding in 1983 came from Community Development Block Grant monies. The Youth Internship Program was expanded to a fourth high school in 1984, and plans call for the addition of one school each year until all seven of the City's high schools are involved.

The Summer Youth Employment Program
Minneapolis' Summer Youth Employment Program has long been a success in placing young residents in jobs, in large measure due to the cooperative relationship which has existed between the city's schools, the local Job Service office and the Minneapolis Employment and Training Program. In recognition of the year-round educational needs of some youths, a recent development in the summer hiring program has been the inclusion of a remedial education component with benchmark testing used as a basis for determining eligibility for work. For most of the participating youths—approximately 60 percent of whom are under nineteen years of age—the primarily public service jobs are their first experiences in a supervised work environment.

The Year-Round Youth Program

Despite one of the lowest school dropout rates in the country—between 12 and 14 percent—a year-round program aimed at this segment of Minneapolis' youth population was initiated in 1983. Viewing the long-term employment prospects of dropouts as integrally tied to their completion of high school, designers of the Year-Round Youth Program made return to a traditional high school or enrollment in an alternative school a condition for participation in both pre-employment and employment phases of the Program.

Organizational Involvement and Funding

Following the lead of the Mayor's office, the city's public education system, the Minneapolis Employment and Training Program and the Chamber of Commerce are the major partners in all three of Minneapolis' youth employment initiatives. The Youth Work Internship Program, with 90 percent of its placements in the private sector, is managed by the Chamber of Commerce and coordinated by both Chamber Staff and school officials. Assessment and testing is performed by the Minneapolis Technical Institute under contract.

Funding for the Internship Program is presently derived from a variety of sources, including $35,000 from a local foundation, the McKnight Foundation, $27,000 from JTPA funds, $10,000 from Chamber of Commerce members and $5,000 from the school system. In the future, the majority of funds for the Program are expected to come from the Chamber and the schools.

The Summer Youth Employment Program and the Year-Round Youth Program are both administered by the Minneapolis Employment and Training Program (METP), the administrative entity for the City's JTPA grant. In the case of the Summer Program, which is funded this year with approximately $1.4 million in JTPA Title II-B funds, $250,000 from the Minnesota State Legislature and small contributions from the school system and private corporations, the state Job Service office provides eligibility certifications, enrollment and job matching services. These services, as well as the summertime remedial education component, are provided in the junior and senior high schools.

In contrast, the Year-Round Youth Program involves thirteen community-based organizations—four of which serve as alternatives schools—and the Chamber of Commerce as the job placement agency. In operation for almost four years, the Year-Round Program is presently funded with $680,000 in JTPA Title II-A money.

Characteristics of The Target Population

As the needs of junior high school students differ from those in high school, and as in-school youths must be addressed differently than dropouts, so too are the targets of Minneapolis' three youth employment initiatives different. While the Internship Program is restricted to high school juniors and seniors enrolled in school, the Summer Program numbers slightly more than half of its participants among the fourteen to fifteen year age group. Owing to the diversity of circumstances which cause youths of varying ages to drop out of school, the Year-Round Program serves school-age as well as older youths.

In each of these programs, at least 50 percent of participating youths are Black (70 percent in the Internship Program), on average 16 percent Southeast Asian (although fully one-quarter of the younger-aged Summer Program participants are refugees), approximately 13 percent White (except the Year-Round Program which numbers 24 percent White), and between 8-9 percent Native Americans. Hispanic youth participation has been quite low, with only 1 percent participation in the Summer Program and 2 percent in the Year-Round Program.

Other characteristics of the target populations include: approximately 50 percent of participants in each program were from families on public assistance, there was somewhat higher female participation in the Internship Program and slightly more males in the Year-Round Program, and at least 10 percent of participants in each program performed below their academic grade level.

Key Elements

The integration of educational and employment components in each of the three Minneapolis programs reflects a "state-of-the-art" approach to the problems confronting many disadvantaged youths. Additionally, efforts to focus services on the most at-risk segments of the JTPA-eligible population reflect the wisdom of targeting limited resources where needs are greatest. Beyond these commonalities, the key elements of each program is presented separately below.

The Youth Work Internship Program

As a school-to-work transitions program, the Internship Program has as its goals: (1) the retention of youths in school, (2) the enhancement of participants' personal growth and (3) the successful preparation of youths for the world of work. In operation almost two years, this program now operates in four of Minneapolis' seven high schools and serves more than 220 high school juniors and seniors. Program and participant criteria for each school are determined by Guidance Committees composed of school administrators and counselors, job service counselors, social workers and CBO and business representatives.

A full range of pre-employment services leading to placement in predominately (90 percent) private sector internships are offered in each school. They include: vocational assessment, orientation sessions, workshops and field trips, basic skills testing, counseling, summer job placement and senior-year curriculum planning assistance. Evaluations of work and school performance are provided, as well as full-time job placement assistance upon graduation. Working closely with the Guidance Committees and school officials, the Chamber of Commerce serves as the placement agency for youths who complete the pre-employment curriculum.

The Summer Youth Employment Program

With the inclusion of a remedial education component, Minneapolis' Summer Program seeks to address the academic regressions which have been documented among many youths during summer vacation periods. The Program begins with a required after-school orientation course in May—the successful completion of which is a pre-condition of summer employment —and tests participants according to academic benchmarks. While passage of the benchmark test enables youths to work twenty hours per week during the summer, failure of one benchmark restricts the number of work hours to fifteen and imposes a six-week, 2-1/2 hours-per-day summer school requirement. Failure of two benchmarks further limits work to ten hours per week and requires five hours a day in summer school for six weeks. The decision of a student not to participate in summer school, if required, precludes employment and results in termination from the Program. (Similar requirements exist for Internship Program participants.)

As noted earlier, the majority of jobs in the Summer Program are in public service agencies, such as parks and recreation programs and day care centers.

The Year-Round Youth Program

Targeted primarily to dropouts, the Year-Round Program attempts to return youths to traditional school settings or to enroll them in alternative schools (see the Chicago case study for an in-depth look at the "alternative" school concept), utilizing employment opportunities as incentives to do so. The school participation requirement is a pre-condition and continued condition of employment until high school equivalency has been achieved.

Community-based organizations, some of which serve as alternative schools, recruit, counsel, prepare and refer participants for employment. The Chamber of Commerce provides two-day "crash course" orientations on employment to new participants. This course addresses the fundamentals of searching for and finding a job in the private sector. If judged "job ready" upon completion of this course, participants are sent on interviews; if judged not to be ready, participants are referred back to the CBO for more work experience, with subsequent reviews every two weeks.

Jobs developed through the Chamber's placement efforts are typically entry-level and part-time, with the main objectives being to provide private sector work experience, a reference, some financial help and an incentive to complete school. Monitoring of participants in the Year-Round Program is handled by the Chamber for the first thirty days and thereafter by the employer and the CBO.

Results

Employment initiatives on behalf of disadvantaged youths, such as the three Minneapolis programs described in this study, are sometimes more meaningfully assessed by their effort than by their results. In the case of Minneapolis, both the quality of effort and the results bear out the success of the three programs.

The Youth Work Internship Program, a main goal of which is to keep youths in school, lost only 3 of its first year's 86 participants. Upon completion of their senior year, more than one-third (30) transitioned into full-time employment, and the other 53 chose to work part-time and continue their education.

The Summer Youth Employment Program served between 1,500 and 2,000 disadvantaged youths through its combined work and summer school format during the summer of 1985. While evaluative data were not yet available as of this writing, program officials note a very low dropout rate from the program and enthusiasm on the part of youth involved in summer jobs.

Finally, the Year-Round Youth Program, targeting the most difficult of youth population segments, dropouts, offers particularly impressive results. Officials report that 81 percent of participants who go through the program are placed in part-time, private sector jobs. Post-placement tracking of one group of participants revealed further that 91 percent have either graduated or at least advanced to the next grade level.

Contributing to such high placement and educational advancements of the dropout group is attributable, in part, to the requirement of remaining in school as a condition of employment. Another factor is the cohesive working relationship between the CBO's, many of whom are located in the neighborhoods of participants, the Chamber of Commerce staff and employers.

A variation of the Year-Round Program which seeks to help older youths (ages eighteen to twenty-one) with employability problems was begun in January of 1985. This variation, called the "Transitional Work Internship Program," involved one-year placements in Minneapolis' city departments, with subsequent training or placement in the private sector. Characteristics of participants in this program include: 90 percent minorities, 60 percent females, about 25 percent having court histories or chemical dependency problems, and an unspecified percentage of teenage parents.

One overall—and most impressive—result of Minneapolis' youth employment initiatives is the fact that, unlike many areas of the country, the city has been able with ease to meet the JTPA performance standard of spending 40 percent of funds for youth. A combination of sensitivity, concern and commitment, matched by competence and strong local leadership, suggests the key to Minneapolis' successes.

For More Information, Contact:

Chip Wells, Coordinator
Program Operations
Minneapolis Employment and
Training Program
Room 310½ City Hall
Minneapolis, MN 55415
(612) 348-4386

ADDRESSING THE DROPOUT PROBLEM BEFORE IT BEGINS
A Program of Prevention and Amelioration

OPERATION SUCCESS
New York, New York

With an officially acknowledged overall dropout rate of 40 percent—and studies suggesting an overall rate as high as 60 percent—New York City has a school dropout problem which is, without a doubt, enormous. Add to this the estimates of a 70 percent dropout rate among Black youths and an 80 percent rate for Hispanic youths and the dimensions of the problem increase. The consequent circumstance in which New York's public school system finds itself is one of serving less than half of the school-age population for which it is responsible.

Beginning in the 1982-83 school year, a program originally sponsored by the New York State Education Department was instituted to address the city's school dropout problem. Entitled "Operation Success," the program was designed to address both dropout prevention and the needs and problems of youths who had already left school.

Of the nearly 2,000 youths served by Operation Success during the 1983-84 school year, all but 80 were potential dropouts still in school, suggesting that solutions to the problem of dropouts lie in reaching students before they leave school. One measure of the program's success is the fact that nearly 92 percent of the 1983-84 participants were either still in school or had graduated. Another measure is the fact that the program has expanded from three high schools in its pilot year to seven in the 1985-86 school year. One junior high school is also participating this year.

Operation Success has been used by the U.S. Department of Health and Human Services as one of four national models for proposals to serve dropout youth.

Background

Operation Success was undertaken in 1982 by a private, nonprofit organization, the Federation Employment and Guidance Service (FEGS), with a grant secured from the Education Department. The first step taken by FEGS was the formation of a task force, comprised of FEGS staff, representatives from the High School and Special Education Divisions of New York City's Board of Education, and representatives from the largest of the city's Teachers' unions, the United Federation of Teachers. The task force established working relationships with the faculties and staffs of the three pilot schools, identifying the particular needs of each school, developing programmatic components and working out logistical issues. An extensive search for program coordinators for each school, as well as for staff sensitive to the needs of dropouts, was conducted by FEGS. Program staffs, as well as school personnel, were provided with a week of initial orientation, with in-service training continuing regularly.

Organizational Involvement and Funding

As noted, Operation Success was begun under the sponsorship of the New York State Education Department, a sponsorship which continued through the second year. The program was designed by FEGS in collaboration with the organizations represented on the task force and, for the first two years, administered by FEGS staff. A number of New York City's social service agencies assist program participants and/or their families with appropriate services based on referrals from the schools. Now in its fourth year, Operation Success is sponsored by the New York City Board of Education and operates in seven high schools and one junior high.

Funding for the program's first two years came from the State Education Department in the amounts of $1.2 million and $1.8 million respectively. With the sponsorship of Operation Success assumed in the 1984-85 year by New York City's Board of Education, the funding level was slightly lower due to a reconfiguration of the program's structure. Funding for the 1985-86 school year is set at $2.4 million.

Characteristics of The Target Population

Data accounting for approximately 95 percent of students participating in Operation Success in 1983-84 indicate the following characteristics of the group:

- approximately 85 percent are between fifteen and nineteen years of age;
- 57.5 percent are Black, 25.6 percent are Hispanic, 12.5 percent White, 2.2 percent Asian and 2.2 percent other;
- 57.4 percent are male and 42.6 percent female;
- 20.5 percent are not native born;
- 13.3 percent of the 795 females are teenage mothers or pregnant on enrollment;
- 37.4 percent come from families receiving public assistance;
- 42.8 percent (of 1,380 surveyed) come from families with incomes of less than $8,000 a year;
- 61 percent (of 1,606 surveyed) come from single parent households; and
- 41.3 percent have never held a job.

Key Elements

Operation Success programs target two distinct segments of New York City's youth population. One segment is the potential dropout who, for a variety of reasons, is prone to leaving school but has not yet done so. The other segment consists of youths who have dropped out of the traditional school setting.

In an effort to address the potential dropout, the programs aim to: 1) develop skills, 2) improve self-awareness and self-direction, 3) encourage formation of career goals and 4) foster appropriate attitudes toward the world of work. For youths who have already left school, the efforts are: 1) to reach out to both the dropout and his/her family, 2) to get the youth back into school, and 3) to assist the returned student in overcoming specific educational and personal hardships.

Indicators of students who are regarded as "high risks" of dropping out are long-term or excessive absenteeism and tardiness. Other indicators of "at-risk" status are behavior problems, past suspensions, histories of dropping out and pregnancy and adjustment problems, some of which are brought on by newness in the country.

Students identified as high risk or at-risk are recruited for participation in the programs in a variety of ways. Open house activities at each school prior to the opening of the school year represents one way of attracting both students and families. Students expressing interest at these open house sessions are then enrolled in the three-week Operation Success Summer Developmental Program on the condition that the student will return to school in the fall. As Operation Success has grown, information about the in-school programs has been conveyed through direct mailings, telephone contact, neighborhood outreach publicity posters and referrals by teachers, counselors and other students.

All students participating in Operation Success programs receive all or some of the following services:

- Initial diagnostic vocational evaluation and functional assessment
- Education internship experience (more than 400 per year)
- Personal and family counseling
- Outreach services
- Vocational skills training at FEGS Vocational Trades School (training offerings include air conditioning, refrigeration and heating repair, major home appliance repair, building maintenance, typewriter repair, jewelry manufacturing and office/business skills. Approximately 500 students participate in these training programs.
- Part-time job development and employment
- Career development services
- Community resource development
- Treatment service
- Referral

To provide these services to students—the appropriate mix of which is determined according to individual needs—ten to twelve staff members worked in each of the participating schools during the first two years of the program. Composition of the staff included case managers, outreach workers, educational internship specialists, job developers, placement coordinators, career development specialists, vocational evaluators, administrative assistants and a rotating community resource specialist. Staff members presented a wide variety of educational and work backgrounds.

Results

As noted in the introduction of this case study, program sites for Operation Success have expanded steadily over the first three years. More significantly, the programs have succeeded in keeping 1,617 of 1,936—83.5 percent—of youths in school during the 1983-84 year, the last for which complete data is available. Another 163— 8.4 percent—have graduated, and others have taken jobs, joined the armed forces or been referred for additional testing and assessment leading to job placement. The program operates at the very cost-effective average of $1,000 per student.

Of the 163 who graduated from Operation Success programs, 74 received a regular high school diploma and 89 a GED. Nearly 36 percent of this group have enrolled in or plan to attend college, another 9 percent intend to continue in vocational or other continuing education programs and 30 percent are employed in full- or part-time jobs.

The "success" of Operation Success in preventing at-risk students from leaving school offers hope for New York's enormous dropout problem. The fact that in 1983-84 almost 95 percent of the programs' participants were youths who had not yet left school—while only 5 percent were actual dropouts who returned—suggests the essentiality of reaching youths before the decision to drop out has been made. It also suggests the need for more and better efforts to attract dropouts back to school, and, for those not likely to return, some alternative means for learning and skill development.

For More Information, Contact:

Rae Linefsky, Senior Vice-President
Educational/Vocational Services
Federation Employment and Guidance
   Service
62 West 14th Street, 7th Floor
New York, NY 10011
(212) 741-6140

AN ALTERNATIVE FOR DROPOUTS
Community-based Centers for Educational and Support Services

THE ALTERNATIVE SCHOOLS NETWORK
Chicago, Illinois

The alienation of disadvantaged young people from traditional education systems is a major factor in the decision of many to drop out of school. Even when other factors, such as pregnancy, delinquency and substance abuse and family problems are the explanation for dropping out, traditional school settings often hold little attraction for dropouts to return. Underlying these circumstances is the fact that, as they become adults, dropouts will experience severe problems related to employability, problems traditionally ameliorated through educations. The need, therefore, is for alternatives to in-school programs which offer quality education in an environment with which dropouts can identify and in which they can learn.

In the city of Chicago, a network of fifty community-based centers offers both quality education and support services designed to meet the special needs of dropouts. Of this network of fifty, all but four centers offer programs leading to a high school diploma or a GED, and nearly half offer "state of the art" competency based education. Chicago's Alternative Schools Network, now in its thirteenth year of operation, serves approximately 2,000 dropout youths each year. Working closely with the local Private Industry Council and the Mayor's Office of Employment and Training, the centers provide a full range of employability development and placement services for jobs in both the public and private sectors.

Background

In response to an alarmingly high dropout rate among Chicago school students—45 percent overall with 14,000 additional dropouts each year—the city's alternative schools formed a network of educational services available throughout the metropolitan area. Formation of the network led to funding from the existent CETA program, the stream of which has continued—and actually increased—under JTPA.

Organizational Involvement and Funding

As community-based organizations, member schools in the network represent a decentralized model of service delivery. For dropout youths who reject the approach offered in the traditional school setting, the "neighborhood" identification of the alternative schools lends both credibility and a comfortable sense of environment. At the same time, the alternative schools are part of a citywide network with ties to Chicago's Private Industry Council and City Hall. Collaborative relationships also exist between network directors and the city's public school administrators.

Financial support for programs offered by the Alternative Schools Network is derived primarily from JTPA Title II-A funds, this year in the amount of $900,000. The introduction of the Comprehensive Competencies Program into nineteen of the fifty schools has been underwritten largely with this PIC grant and $450,000 in support from the MacArthur, Woods, Ford and Joyce Foundations. Another source of funds, $420,000 to be exact—is the Title XX social service fund which supports counseling for participants enrolled in alternative school programs. In addition, the schools raise as much as $1 million each year from a variety of sources.

Characteristics of The Target Population

The Network serves sixteen-to-twenty-one-year-old out-of-school youth, all of whom must be JTPA eligible, with 60 percent of the youths between sixteen and eighteen while 40 percent are nineteen to twenty-one.

Seventy percent of participants are Black, 20 percent are Hispanic and 10 percent are White. Of the 55 percent females enrolled, 20-25 percent are teen parents. Between 15 and 20 percent have criminal justice histories. The average reading level at the time of enrollment is fifth to seventh grade. Overall, group characteristics are quite similar to those in New York programs and in other community programs throughout the country.

Key Elements

In the eight to ten months in which participants on the average are in the Alternative School programs, they receive educational services leading to, in most cases, a high school diploma or GED. As noted, in nineteen of the schools, computer-based comprehensive competencies provide the curriculum structure.

The CCP concept offers an individualized self-paced instructional system employing the assistance of computers. The CCP functions as a complement to daily teacher-instructed courses in basic academic skills, serving 40-45 youths at any given time.

In addition to educational services, career counseling and job readiness training, job development and placement services are also provided. Placements are made in both public and private sector jobs—part-time positions while participants are in school—most of which are entry level positions designed to impart work experience, promote good work habits and provide necessary income. Performance on the job is monitored by job developers for the approximately 35 percent of participants who hold jobs. Use of the Targeted Jobs Tax Credit is promoted to employers by job developers, though the necessary amount of "selling" of TJTC is not always possible and small employers are reticent to apply.

Results

Of the 2,000 youths served by Alternative Schools Network in the past year, 35 percent (700) were placed in part-time jobs while enrolled in the program. For graduates of the program, the placement rate into full-time jobs was 40 percent, with another 10 percent placed in part-time work.

As a program to re-engage school dropouts in the learning process, the success of Chicago's Alternative Schools Network—one of the largest organizations of its kind in the country—is reflected in the statistic that fully 25 percent of participants have gone on to receive a high school diploma. Future prospects appear even brighter as Comprehensive Competencies Programs are more widely utilized, with expectations of two- to three-grade level advancements for each eight- to ten-month participation period. With nineteen out of a national total of ninety-four CCP Learning Centers in operation, Chicago's Alternative Schools Network is a virtual laboratory for demonstrating the effectiveness of the CCP approach to remediation and learning. As a neighborhood-based program, the Network also serves as a model approach for addressing the needs of inner-city dropout youths.

For More Information, Contact:

Jack West, Director
Alternative Schools Network
1105 West Laurence Avenue, Suite 210
Chicago, IL 60640
(312) 728-4030

WORK EXPERIENCE AND LEARNING IN A COMMUNITY SERVICE SETTING
The Conservation Corps Concept

THE SACRAMENTO LOCAL CONSERVATION CORPS
Sacramento, California

For disadvantaged youths preparing to enter the labor force, opportunities for viable work experience are often critical to both a successful entry and continuation in employment. For youths suffering from basic skills deficiences, there is the need to combine work experience with remediation instruction and guidance. One approach to providing this combination which has received increasing attention in recent years is the youth conservation and service corps.

Currently thirty-five states and localities have youth corps in operation, and many others have proposals under consideration. At the national level, Congress passed legislation in 1984 authorizing the establishment of an American Conservation Corps; the President chose not to sign the bill into law. A similar scenario may again play out in 1985.

Of the states which have adopted the conservation and service corps concept, California has been among the leaders in providing opportunities of this kind for economically disadvantaged young persons to learn and gain valuable work experience performing needed public services. The success of the statewide program, begun in 1976, has led to similar initiatives at the local level, of which Sacramento's Local Conservation Corps is one. In only its first year of operation, the Sacramento program has gained wide visibility and received praise for its efforts to target neigh-borhoods of high unemployment among ethnic and minority youths.

Background

Sacramento's Local Conservation Corps evolved from the successful experience, in 1983, of a summer corps program run by the local Small Business Administration with funds from the California Conservation Corps. The work and learning experience gained by participants in the summer program pointed to the value of the conservation corps concept and also to its need on a year-round basis. Organized by the President of the local SBA Board, a broad-based group of community residents worked for a year to turn the idea into reality. In November of 1984, the Sacramento Local Conservation Corps was incorporated and, in January of this year, its doors were opened.

Organizational Involvement and Funding

As a non-profit organization, the Sacramento Corps is governed by a Board of Directors composed of community residents, representative of large and small businesses, the Chamber of Commerce and the Sacramento City Council. Housed on the campus of the Consumnes River College which provides both high school equivalency classes and college tuition assistance to corps members, the Corps also benefits from the involvement of local school districts, local and state Park Services, the Water Resources Department, the Sacramento Employment and Training Agency, and the Sacramento Economic Development Department.

Funding for the Sacramento Corps comes from a supplement to the California Conservation Corps' (CCC) budget added in late 1984. The 1.2 million appropriation established non-residential programs with an educational component in neighborhoods with high concentrations of ethnic and minority youths experiencing severe unemployment. Much of the 1.2 million has been subgranted by the CCC to local corps programs.

The Sacramento Corps received $285,000 to which must be matched 25 percent or $71,500. Thus far, approximately $20,000 has been raised through local business contributions, and a $30,000 contract is expected soon from Sacramento Employment and Training Agency to fund the educational component, CPR training and other programs. As this contract would be funded with JTPA monies, its receipt would mark a significant breakthrough for conservation corps programs. The remainder of this year's local match is derived from project reimbursements and fees for service rendered by corpsmembers. Next year's funding plan calls for assistance from California foundations and increased support from corporations and other private sources.

Characteristics of The Target Population

Recruitment of Sacramento's corpsmembers is targeted to areas marked by poverty and high levels of unemployment. Characteristically, these areas are populated largely by ethnic and minority popula-tions whose youth suffer from inordinate levels of joblessness. The results of such a targeting strategy have yielded a 98 percent JTPA-eligible corps enrollment, composed of 70 percent Black enrollees, 15 percent Hispanic, 7-10 percent Whites, 5 percent Native Americans and 2-3 percent Asians.

At present only 24 percent of corpsmembers are female, an imbalance which is being addressed actively. Approximately one-third (18) of the current 52 corpsmember class have received some form of public assistance, 3 are teenage parents and about 10 percent have had some involvement with the law. Testing by the college upon enrollment has revealed an average reading level equivalent to the seventh grade. Prospective corpsmembers must be between the ages of eighteen and twenty-three.

Key Elements

As a non-residential, urban conservation corps program, the Sacramento initiative is geared to serve 100 or more youths annually, with an average of 50 corpsmembers enrolled at any one time. While participation can be for as long as one year, the average length of service—based on the experience of other corps programs—is five and one-half months.

Corps members work on a variety of conservation, development and maintenance projects on public lands for city and county agencies, community colleges and nonprofit organizations. Work performed includes stream clearance, construction of fire breaks, play equipment and cement work. Use of corps resources to respond to emergencies is expected in the near future, as flood emergency training has already been incorporated and forest fire-fighting will soon be added.

The Sacramento Corps is composed of five crews of ten to twelve members each who work under supervisors four days a week at the minimum wage. The fifth day is spent in unpaid mandatory education and training, the educational component being geared toward obtaining a high school diploma or college-level study in the Consumnes River College's cooperative education program.

Participation in the Corps requires hard work and motivation on the part of members. The high standards set by the program are expected to be met by all participants; those who do not meet them are terminated to make room for others.

Two features of the Sacramento youth initiative are especially important as considerations in the design of a model conservation corps. One is the close connection of the Consumnes River College— indeed the Corps is housed on campus— as an excellent educational environment for youths, some of whom may not have considered post-secondary education previously. The other feature is the acquisition of JTPA funds for training components of the Corps program. As JTPA differs significantly from CETA in its restrictions on traditional work experience activities, the combined training and work experience

provided to participants serves a dual purpose.

Results

As noted, the Sacramento Local Conservation Corps is in its initial year, thus results as of this writing are incomplete. Of the 31 corpsmembers who have gone on after their average five and one-half month stints, 23 who had originally returned to school in the program's mandatory education component are still in school elsewhere. Six of this group have found full-time jobs, one with a sponsor of the Corps for whom he had performed work as a corpsmember and three others as a direct result of assistance from Corps staff.

An audit of the Sacramento program by the CCC resulted in a rating of excellent.

For More Information, Contact:

Ron Espinoza, Executive Director or
Gary VanDorst, Assistant Director
Sacramento Local Conservation Corps
40 Consumnes River College
8401 Center Parkway
Sacramento, CA 95823
(916) 423-3139

SERVING THE NEEDS OF YOUTH IN SMALL COMMUNITIES
A Comprehensive Approach to Education, Training and Support

THE YAKIMA VALLEY OIC CENTER
Yakima, Washington

Limitations on resources, service deliverers and jobs create special barriers to disadvantaged youths in small communities. Creative and effective approaches to serving the needs of youth can, on the other hand, maximize resources and generate support from many elements of the community. In some cases, a sharing of responsibilities and resources by more than one small community can yield collective benefits to youths and their communities.

In Yakima Valley, Washington, a fourteen-year-old Opportunities Industrialization Center (OIC) provides educational, skill training, job placement and other services to over 1,000 young people a year in a two-county area of small communities. Through its four youth training centers and one satellite office, the Yakima Valley OIC operates Educational Clinics, an Alternative High School, a Summer Youth Employment Program and a "Hire One Youth" Program targeted to private sector employers. In addition, the Center operates special programs for ex-offenders, single female heads-of-households and adults, some of which involve youth and adults collaboratively. Job Clubs, tutorial services and recreational activities are still other dimensions of the OIC comprehensive services program.

Background

Declining opportunities in Yakima Valley's major industries, food processing and tim-ber, and the chronic problems associated with seasonal employment and a migrant workforce inspired the director of the area's community center in 1971 to explore the possibilities of establishing an OIC program in the valley. With the technical assistance of the National OIC and an employment and training contract for $156,000, the Yakima Valley OIC became a reality. Having overcome many problems related to the predominantly rural makeup of the valley and the fact that its service area covers two counties, the Center is today the preeminent service provider in the valley operating on an annual budget of nearly $3.5 million. Its Executive Director is the same man who conceived of and founded the Center fourteen years ago.

Organizational Involvement and Funding

An OIC program in the traditional sense, the Yakima Valley Center enjoys close working relationships with the JTPA Tri-Valley Service Delivery Area Consortium, the Yakima and Kittitas County School Districts and the Yakima Valley Community College. The school districts have contributed significantly to the Center's educational curriculum development as has the college, which also provides English-as-a-Second-Language (ESL) classes.

Close relationships also exist with private industry and unions in the valley for both youth and adult dislocated worker initiatives. Additionally, OIC serves as co-ordinator of a court-related project in which offenders perform community service work at the Center. Ties are also maintained with various social service agencies, primarily for referrals. And, as a member of the Chamber of Commerce, OIC collaborates with other members for job development and enhancement of skills training programs.

The nearly $3.5 million annual budget reflects the total amount of a number of contracts and grants. They include:

- Community Services Block Grant funds
- Tri-Valley SDA Consortium funds (for Job Clubs, Summer Youth Employment and Dislocated Worker Programs
- State Department of Public Instruction money (for the Educational Clinic)
- Local public school systems (for the Alternative High School)
- Washington State Commission for Vocational Education (for the Vocational Offenders Program and Vocational Business Program)
- State Employment Security Department
- Tacoma Urban League (Highway Construction Project)
- State Department of Community Development (Energy Assistance and Weatherization Projects)
- Local business and community contributions.

Characteristics of The Target Population

Ranging from fourteen to twenty-one years of age, the group served reflects the overall makeup of Yakima Valley's population. Slightly more than half the participants (54 percent) are White, 28 percent are Hispanic, 9 percent Black, 8 percent Native American and 1 percent Asian. Sixty per-cent of participants are female, 40 percent male.

An estimated 15 percent are teenage parents, 8-10 percent have had some involvement with the law, and 60 percent of Hispanic participants have limited knowledge of English. Half of all youths served are out of school and 90 percent of them high school ages; 5 percent have graduated and another 5 percent have GEDs. The average reading and computational levels of the group are between seventh and eighth grade.

Key Elements

The combination of education, skills training, placement, supportive services and special programs creates a truly comprehensive approach to serving Yakima Valley's youth. With four training centers and a satellite office, OIC's access to the dispersed population of the two counties is maximized and ties to local employers are significantly closer than they might otherwise be. Further, the fact that OIC programs address adult as well as youth needs means fuller understanding of the area's problems and greater continuity in service delivery.

In addressing migrant as well as year-round population needs, the Center tailors training programs in any number of fields, among them: computer literacy, computer programming, word processing, typing, accounting, bookkeeping, sales, cashiering, small business management and building maintenance. In addition to skills training, on-the-job training and work experience placements are developed, in part through the Center's own revenue-generating businesses, including a thrift store and two snack bars.

OIC's year-round Educational Clinic serves approximately 135 high school dropouts between sixteen and twenty-one years old with a prescriptive educational program of academic, motivational and career development services. The Alternative High School, a cooperative program involving the Yakima School System, provides intensive counseling, classroom training, vocational explorations, GED preparation and credit toward a high school diploma. For the large number of Hispanic enrollees whose English abilities are limited, the Yakima Valley Community College provides tuition-free ESL classes.

The many other programs offered by OIC, including Summer Youth Employment, Hire One Youth, etc., ensure flexibility in serving the specific types of needs of the area's youth (and adult) populations.

Results

Of the more than 1,000 youths served in 1984 by the Yakima Valley OIC—an average of 635 participating at any one time—62 percent were placed in jobs. Of this group four-fifths were placed in full-time employment, the other fifth in part-time positions as they continued their educations. Private sector placements accounted for 47 percent of all jobs, while combined public and nonprofit positions represented 53 percent. Data on individual components of OIC comprehensive program mix are obtainable from the Center.

For More Information, Contact:

Henry Beaucharro, Executive Director or
Esther Huey, Operations Director
Yakima Valley Opportunities Industrialization Center
1201 Fruitvale Boulevard
Yakima, WA 98902
(509) 248-6751

HELP FOR THE TEENAGE PARENT
Serving the Special Needs of Pregnant Adolescents and Adolescent Parents

THE NEW FUTURES SCHOOL
Albuquerque, New Mexico

Problems associated with adolescent pregnancy and teenage parenthood—ranging from ones related to the health and well-being of mother and child to educational, skill, and personal development problems—comprise one of the most serious human resource dilemmas facing society today. As the consequences of these problems fall predominantly on women, many of whom are single heads of households, teenage pregnancy and parenthood contribute immeasureably to the feminization of poverty. In turn, the prospects for cyclical poverty—i.e. poverty passed from generation to generation—are greatest among families which begin under such circumstances.

Out of the basement of the Albuquerque YWCA in 1970, an effort was launched to address the needs and problems of young mothers and mothers to be. Responding to dual concerns of health problems and expulsions from school, YWCA volunteers built a program which would ultimately become the New Futures School. Today, the New Futures School assists approximately 700 persons a year, providing multiple services to pregnant adolescents, adolescent parents, including fathers, and children. The School's two main programs—one a perinatal program, the other a program for young parents—are recognized throughout the country as models of what can be done on behalf of one of society's most at-risk segments.

Background

At the outset, cooperation between the Albuquerque school system and the YWCA center was limited. Commitment on the part of the schools went no further than acknowledgement of credit for classes taught at the Center by certified teachers. Between 1970 and 1976, the involvement and financial commitments of the school system increased as the program grew, culminating, in 1976, with the system's assumption of primary responsibility for the program. At that same time, a new community-based organization, New Futures, Inc., was formed to maintain community involvement and support. In addition to serving as the link between the schools and the community, New Futures, Inc., provides technical assistance to other New Mexico communities and programs throughout the country.

Organizational Involvement and Funding

The New Futures School is an alternative school model within the Albuquerque public system. In addition to the support of New Futures, Inc., the School's programs and services receive contributions from a variety of other organizations. Among these are: the League of United Latin American Citizens, the Albuquerque Public Health Department, the local WIC Nutrition Program, the University of New Mexico

Maternity and Infant Care Project, the University of New Mexico School of Medicine's Family Practice Department and Programs for Children. Community involvement includes a Vocational Advisory Committee, a board of community volunteers and individual volunteers who provide support to School students.

Reflecting the commitment of Albuquerque's schools to the needs of pregnant adolescents and adolescent parents, $788,000 of a total of nearly $1.1 million came from the Systems Operational fund in 1984. The second largest source of funds comes from New Futures, Inc., which raised $151,000 in corporate and foundation and individual contributions, as well as some vendor payments for day care centers. JTPA funds, under an "Exemplary Program" grant, totaled $63,000 and the New Mexico Department of Human Services contributed roughly $82,000.

Characteristics of The Target Population

Perhaps the most telling characteristic of the New Futures School target group is the participation level of single women. In the Perinatal Program, 91 percent of the adolescent women are single; in the Young Parents Program, the rate is 73 percent.

The disruptive impact on the educational development of teen parents is suggested in dropout rates of the two groups. Among pregnant adolescents in the Perinatal Program, the dropout rate is one-third; in the Young Parents Program, the rate more than doubles to 72 percent.

Women in the fifteen to eighteen age group represent 86 percent of all participants when the age statistics for both programs are averaged. With respect to ethnic background, slightly more than half (53 percent) of the women are Hispanic, approximately one-quarter (24 percent) are Anglo, 15 percent are Native American, 6.5 percent are Black and 1.5 percent "other". This is again an average for the two programs.

Key Elements

The Perinatal and Young Parents programs offer educational, health, counseling, vocational and child care services to pregnant adolescents and adolescent parents. In the Perinatal Program, a young woman enters at some point in her pregnancy and remains until the end of the semester in which her child is born. Women can be served only for one pregnancy. The Young Parents Center serves school age mothers and fathers who cannot successfully participate in a regular school program in the year(s) following the birth of a child. Participants many remain in the Center's programs as long as their need exists, provided they show steady progress toward a diploma or GED. In some cases, individual contracts are used to specify expectations and measures of progress.

Educational services in both programs include high school academic classes, special education, classes to prepare a young mother for caring for herself during pregnancy and afterwards, vocational instruction and classes in parenting and child development. All educational programs offer credit toward graduation or a GED, and most are individually paced. Close contact is maintained with students' previous schools to facilitate smooth transition to and from the New Futures School.

Health services include individual counseling, group health instruction and nutrition counseling. Participation in the group health instruction and parenting classes are required in both programs. The health status of children in the day care centers is also part of the health staff's responsibilty.

The University of New Mexico's School of Medicine operates a free weekly prenatal clinic at the School, as well as a Family Practice Clinic for which sliding-scale fees are charged. A weekly WIC Clinic and a monthly Well-Child Clinic are also part of the New Futures School's health services.

Vocational counseling of individuals and groups, as well as referral to social service providers and follow-up by School staff, represent another category of School services. Counseling sessions may involve fathers, grandparents or entire families.

Employability training and vocational awareness classes stress job-finding and job-keeping skills for mothers whose children are at least three months old. Upon successful completion of these classes, students are placed in subsidized private sector jobs. Keeping one's job is conditioned on the student remaining in a Jobs Training class for one semester and continued success in three other classes.

The New Futures School also operates an outreach program for school-alienated youths in low-income neighborhoods. Project Redirection, in which community volunteers work one-on-one with pregnant and parenting teens, and a pregnancy prevention program are also operated, sometimes involving students in presentations. As noted above, the School also provides technical assistance in other parts of New Mexico and the country, using books written by staff and a video tape produced by New Futures, Inc.

Results

Since the initial efforts of the YWCA volunteers began fifteen years ago, 3,150 women have been served though the Peri-natal Program. The Young Parents Center, opened in October, 1979, has served 577 young parents, most of them mothers.

A major follow-up study conducted in 1981 found, impressively, that 92 percent of New Futures School students had high school diplomas or were still in school. This achievement rate contrasts sharply with national figures showing less than half of school-age mothers graduating from high school.

Also impressive is the School's success in reducing the incidence of repeat pregnancies to less than one-third of the national rates for teenage pregnancies after one year (6-8 percent versus 18-25 percent). Health problems for children of School students have also proved less serious.

Three elements are cited by New Futures School staff as keys to the success of School programs. One is the comprehensive nature of services in education, health, counseling, child care, and employment. Another is coordination of services, whereby services operate in conjunction with and in support of each other. And the third is a caring, nurturing environment in which young pregnant women and young parents can learn and grow.

For More Information, Contact:

Caroline Gaston, Program Coordination
New Futures School
2120 Louisiana Boulevard, N.E.
Albuquerque, NM 87110
(505) 883-5680

OVERCOMING SPECIAL BARRIERS
Skills Training For Ethnic Minorities

THE CENTER FOR EMPLOYMENT TRAINING
San Jose, California

In the several case studies preceding this one, an array of problems, barriers and special needs affecting disadvantaged youth have been discussed. Indeed, to be young and economically disadvantaged is to face potentially several obstacles to educational and skill development, employment and, ultimately, self-sufficiency. For Hispanic Americans, as well as others to whom English is not a native language, potentially multiple and complex problems are compounded by language difficulties. Cultural distinctions too play a role in making the assimilation into mainstream American life more burdensome for some than for others.

Addressing the education, skill training and human development needs of Hispanics, Asians, Pacific Islanders and other minorities is the mission of the Center for Employment Training (CET) in San Jose, California. The Center's goal is to place both youths and adults in well-paying, unsubsidized jobs in the private sector. In 1984 CET's open-entry, open-exit programs served 1,737 clients, 588 of whom were youths and all of whom were disadvantaged.

Background

In early 1967, a group of residents from the East San Jose "barrio" met to formulate a plan for providing skill training and development services to their poor and unemployed neighbors. Conditions in the barrio were so bad that residents called the area "Sal Si Puedes," meaning "Get out if you can." The group, meeting for the first time, adopted a new phrase for the neighborhood, "Si Se Puede," or "It can be done." With this belief, volunteer projects—including fund-raising events—were undertaken and plans for staffing a grassroots program were developed.

After consultations with a nearby OIC Center, the staff began a program to train fifteen students in machine shop work. The program developed into a full-fledged OIC Center and remained so until 1976, when its affiliation with OIC was ended in order to establish an autonomous, southwestern identity. In the nearly ten years since the Center for Employment Training was established, the number of CET programs has grown to thirty, operating in communities covering seven southwestern states. From their humble beginning in East San Jose's barrio in 1967, CET programs have gone on to train and place over 31,000 people in unsubsidized employment.

Organizational Involvement and Funding

The involvement of the private sector— small businesses as well as large industries—has been the most important element in CET's success. Relationships with as many as 150 private employers provide opportunities for employment, as well as representation on CET's Industrial Advisory Board. Over the past eighteen years, this Board has supported the Center by assisting in curriculum development, industrial orientation and fund raising.

CET's many relationships with public agencies provide the major share of the $3,339,000 budget for San Jose and Santa Clara County Center. The largest single share of funds comes from a JTPA contract totaling $1,920,000. In addition to youth and adult training support, JTPA funds also support dislocated worker services and training for refugees. Other sources of funding include: the California Office of Vocational Education, the California State Employment Development Department, U.S. Department of Labor's Farmworker and Rural Employment Program and Women's Bureau, the Rockefeller Foundation and the Ford Motor Company.

CET also maintains close working relationships with the Santa Clara County Office of Education and the U.S. Department of Education for input into its educational component. Other ties are to the state's Community Services Block Grant and Energy Crisis Intervention Programs, both of which are coordinated by the California Office of Economic Opportunities.

Characteristics of The Target Population

Of the 588 youth trainees enrolled in CET programs in 1984, 62 percent were school dropouts, 12 percent having dropped out at 8th grade level or below. Ninety-six percent had incomes below the poverty level and were unemployed at the time of enrollment.

Hispanic enrollees accounted for 76 percent of the total youth group, 8 percent were Asian or Pacific Islanders, 8 percent were White, 6 percent were Black and 2 percent were Native Americans or Alaskan Indians.

Males represented 58 percent of CET's enrollment, females 42 percent. Thirty-eight percent of participants were AFDC recipients and 20 percent were single parents. Nearly one-quarter (23 percent) were limited in their English-speaking capabilities.

Key Elements

The CET program structure integrates four components into a comprehensive service approach to the needs of disadvantaged youths. The four components are: skills training, education, English-as-a-Second-Language and counseling. In addition, orientation in Spanish as well as English is conducted by Training Team Staff members, most of whom are bilingual. Assistance to Asian enrollees is expanding to meet the needs of this group, particularly those of refugees.

CET skills training is individualized, self-paced, task-oriented and competency-based. Fully equipped workshops simulate actual industry conditions. Occupations for which training is offered include: computer operations, electronics, automotive mechanics, production machine operations, data entry, word processing, shipping and receiving, electro-mechanical assembly, micro assembly, accounting/bookkeeping and building and facilities maintenance.

Training units consist of Instructors/ Counselors who teach both theory and "hands on" training, as well as remedial math and English related to day-to-day training. Instructors/Counselors are drawn directly from private industry, specifically from industries which are determined by analysis to offer the best possible job opportunities in the area. Also part of the Training Team are Support Counselors and Job Developers, the latter of whom are CET's main contacts with private employers. The role of Support Counselors is to promote the personal development of enrollee and to make referrals to social service providers. Free child care is provided to trainers through the recent incorporation of a Montessori Child Development Center.

With the increased spending requirement for youth programs under JTPA, CET expanded its service and programmatic offering to accomodate more serious cases of need among San Jose's youth population. A major element of this expansion was a special remediation program for high school dropouts in need of more intensive remediation than the standard training curriculum provided. Part of California's technical high schools program, CET's technical high school serves these dropout youths through diploma-granting remedial programs. This program is run and staffed by the County Office of Education, and serves twenty-five to thirty students at a time.

Results

The Manpower Demonstration Research Corporation, in appraising the CET Program, found that aside from the Army, the Job Corps and a training program in Pittsburgh, no other organization so incorporates and integrates academic learning into skill training. The underlying principle is to teach what is needed to obtain a skill; other programs, leading to diplomas or GEDs are encouraged but are considered ancillary to actual skills training.

With its origins in the barrio, CET has always been a major contributor to the development of San Jose's Hispanic population. Today more than three-quarters of the Center's enrollees are from the Hispanic community. Another 8 percent are either Asian or Pacific Islanders. The success of CET's skills training programs is reflected in their ability to have placed 70 percent of Hispanic enrollees and 79 percent of Asian and Pacific Islanders. Similarly high rates have been attained for Blacks, Whites and Native American youths.

CET's work with dropout youths has been equally impressive, resulting in an average 67 percent placement rate for this hard-to-employ group. The overall placement rate for CET's program in 1984 was 72 percent.

As an indication of CET's long-term consistency, since 1967 over 31,000 individuals have been trained and placed in unsubsidized jobs at an average cost of $3,643 per placement.

For More Information, Contact:

Robert Johnston, Director of Planning
Russell Tershy, Executive Director
Center for Employment Training
425 South Market Street
San Jose, CA 95113
(408) 287-7924

Chapter 4

HARD-TO-EMPLOY ADULTS
Efforts at Structural Solutions

HARD-TO-EMPLOY ADULTS
Efforts at Structural Solutions

Single female heads-of-households (many of whom became parents while still youths themselves), the long-term unemployed, the homeless and other adults whose lack of skills, poor work histories or personal problems make them difficult to employ share similarly disadvantaged circumstances. Yet each group requires discretely tailored and sometimes multiple efforts to ameliorate its employment problems.

The case studies of local initiatives to help "hard-to-employ" adults reflect the many distinctions in the problems and needs of this population. Sensitivity to personal circumstances and tailoring efforts to meet individual needs are characteristics of each of the initiatives.

Baltimore, Maryland's "OPTIONS" program, a local alternative to the federal government's WIN Program, is the first case study of Chapter 4. Funded as one of Maryland's two "Employment Initiatives" Projects, the Baltimore approach involves individualized employment services to AFDC (women) and AFDC-U (men) recipients in an effort to prepare them for unsubsidized employment. Job Search assistance, public sector work experience, training and state-of-the-art grant diversion techniques form the core of "OPTIONS" sequential service mix.

Skills Training for Entry into the Private Sector (STEPS), a Denver, Colorado initiative, addresses the employment needs of that city's AFDC population, though it differs from the Baltimore program in its greater emphasis on skills training. Voluntary participation on the part of AFDC clients, tailoring of training to the specific needs of private sector employers, and the active involvement of a Business Advisory Council are the key features of the Denver initiative.

In San Antonio, Texas, linking the employment needs of that city's unskilled adult population to a major economic development project has produced benefits to both that population and the project's major employer. At the heart of the effort was the establishment of the SER Learning Center which provided ESL, Adult Basic Education (ABE) and GED instruction, as well as pre-employment and post-placement services. Local residents continue to be hired for openings at the Control Data Corporation's subsidiary through the use of "First Source" hiring agreements.

The emergence of "First Source" hiring agreements between cities and recipients of economic development assistance has much to do with the early successes of this initiative in Portland, Oregon. The City has entered into "First Source" agreements for seven years now, with more than 600 economically disadvantaged Portlanders benefiting from employment.

Addressing the immediate needs of long-term unemployed city residents is the focus of the Work Opportunities Program in Minneapolis, Minnesota. The program, which combines community service employment, On-the-Job Training (OJT) and transitional part-time jobs in serving the truly neediest, was originally proposed by a local foundation and developed by Minneapolis' mayor. The effectiveness of this local initiative is evidenced by the fact that it was later adopted as the model for a statewide program.

The sixth case study in Chapter 4 examines a two-phase project aimed at employing the homeless in San Francisco, California. In the first phase, individuals were placed in public service positions; the second sought to provide on-the-job training opportunities in the public, private and non-profit sectors. (The San Francisco experience is instructive for other communities grappling with the problem of homelessness.)

Creating employment opportunities within city government for economically disadvantaged residents of Tampa, Florida is the objective of the Mayor's On-the-Job Training (OJT) Program. A local version of the old Public Service Employment Program under CETA, the Tampa program uses city tax revenues and targets ten percent of entry-level municipal jobs for participants. The Mayor's OJT Program also helps the City meet its Equal Employment Opportunity (EEO) requirements, as most participants are women and minorities.

FROM WELFARE TO WORK:
A Local Government Approach

THE OPTIONS PROGRAM
Baltimore, Maryland

Since 1982, the City of Baltimore has operated an effective program of employability development and job placement for poor and long-term unemployed adults. Managed by two city departments in conjunction with the state Department of Human Resources, the OPTIONS Program is a local alternative to the WIN Program. In contrast to the standard WIN Program, Baltimore's OPTIONS Program offers a broader base of resources and greater coordination of services to meet the needs of hard-to-employ adults. By the end of 1985, OPTIONS will have provided more than 3,600 clients with individualized employment services, with an average placement rate of 75 percent.

Background

The OPTIONS Program arose as a joint State of Maryland and City of Baltimore initiative to develop more effective approaches to employing welfare recipients. Discussions began in 1980 concerning alternatives to what was regarded as the "punitive" approach of traditional workfare programs, which characteristically offer little chance for long-term employment or growth. The product of those discussions was a new, state-sponsored "Employment Initiatives" Project funded through WIN as a demonstration program.

Targeted to Maryland's highest unemployment areas, one of the first two "Initiatives" was undertaken in the city of Baltimore in the Fall of 1982. At that time Baltimore's overall unemployment rate was 11.3 per cent.

With the transfer of both authority and resources from the state-run WIN agency to the Baltimore Mayor's Office of Manpower Resources (MOMR), this "Initiative" became a local government program and was named "OPTIONS". The credibility and reputation of MOMR as an innovative and effective local agency were factors in the state's agreement to make such a transfer.

Organizational Involvement and Funding

OPTIONS is a joint project of the Baltimore City Department of Social Services (DSS), the City's Office of Manpower Resources (OMR) (part of Baltimore's Neighborhood Progress Administration) and the Maryland Department of Human Resources (DHR). The state agency contracts with OMR to run OPTIONS, with DSS handling WIN client registration and selection for participation in OPTIONS. DSS also makes referrals of program-ready clients to OMR for training and placements and provides support services such as transportation and child care.

Funding for the OPTIONS Program in 1985 comes from four principal sources, the sources and amounts of which are as follows:

WIN Demonstration Program (Title IV-C)	$499,315
AFDC Administrative Funds (Title IV-A)	$140,561
Job Training Partnership Act	$in-kind
AFDC Grant Payment Diversion	$110,000
	$749,876

Characteristics of the Target Population

While replacing the standard WIN program, OPTIONS retained the WIN criteria for participation. Thus, the target population was all AFDC-U recipients (male heads of households below the poverty line) and regular AFDC recipients (female heads of households) with children over five years of age. As is the case in standard WIN programs, registration for OPTIONS is mandatory for these AFDC recipients.

Of the registered group, nearly one quarter—23 percent—are designated for deferral or "holding" status, effectively exempted from participation in the program. Reasons for this designation include family, health and/or medical problems, the employed status of an individual at the time of registration, or enrollment in school or skills training programs. For the 77 percent of registrants deemed eligible, participation in OPTIONS is mandatory.

Characteristics of participants in Baltimore's OPTIONS Program include: 75 percent participation by females; 63 percent of participants are Black, 35 percent are White; 58 percent have less than a high school education, with a participant average of 10.5 school years; and 73 percent are under thirty-five years of age.

Within the AFDC population, approximately 86 percent are regular AFDC recipients, the remainder receive AFDC-U payments. Nearly half of this population has been receiving AFDC for more than two years, having not held a job for at least that long.

Key Elements

OPTIONS provides a variety of employability development and training services to its client population in an attempt to prepare individuals for and place them in unsubsidized jobs. The focus of the Program's placement efforts is on long-term employment opportunities, where possible, above the entry level. While its mix of services and placement strategy resembles the approaches of other programs, the keys to OPTIONS success have been its flexible sequencing of program activities and its individualized employability plans.

Major components of the OPTIONS program are:

Job Search Assistance

Rendered through classroom-style workshops, job search assistance focuses on job-hunting techniques and supervised job search and is utilized by virtually every OPTIONS participant. In June 1984, this component was expanded from three weeks to two months.

Public Sector Work Experience

Participants are placed in public and nonprofit agencies for thirteen-week periods to develop work skills, positive work habits, and employment history and references.

Occupational and Remedial Training

Skills training in specific occupational categories and/or remedial education services are provided through this component.

Grant Diversion

Once job-ready, participants are matched with private sector employers for contracted on-the-job training at prevailing wages. Participants' AFDC benefits are diverted to employers to offset 50 percent of the training wages. (Maryland is one of eight states under federal waiver to divert AFDC funds.)

Results

In its first two years of operation, OPTIONS (in 1984 called OPTIONS II) has served 1121 clients on AFDC and AFDC-U incomes (593 in FY'82; 528 in FY'83). More than twice that number—2,547—have been registered. However, the program-eligible segment of the group is, at any given time, fractional. The relativity of the participation rate is also determined by the resource capacity of the Program—funding, manpower, etc.

With respect to participation in components of the Program, 84 percent received job search assistance, 49 percent pre-employment training and 47 percent work experience. The grant diversion (on-the-job-training component which is still an evolving concept) has served approximately 10 percent of total participants. The average hourly wage of OJT participants was $5.17 for men and $4.01 for women.

Baltimore's OPTIONS Program embodies a state-of-the-art approach to assisting hard-to-employ adults. At its heart is a flexible and sequential mix of services tailored to the individual needs of clients. A caseload one-third the size of WIN case managers allows OPTIONS staff more and better-quality time to assess, monitor and counsel clients. And, as its approach to grant diversion is more fully developed and expanded, OPTIONS will increasingly provide assistance-dependent families and individuals with a viable alternative to the poverty and despair of long-term unemployment.

For More Information, Contact:

David Siegel
Office of Welfare Employment Policy
Department of Human Resources
2122 W. Pratt Street
Baltimore, Maryland 21223
(301) 383-2166

"STEPS" TO ENDING DEPENDENCY
Skills Training For Public Assistance Recipients

THE STEPS PROGRAM
Denver, Colorado

A second example of employment and training services targeted to public assistance recipients is Denver's STEPS Program, the acronym for Skills Training for Entry into the Private Sector. While similar to Baltimore's OPTIONS Programs in its linkage with the local WIN Program, STEPS is more training-intensive in its approach, emphasizing skill development in high-demand occupations. The Program is structured around a short-term, flexible curriculum which addresses employer expectations and positive work habits in addition to skills training.

In the two-and-one-half years in which it operated—January 1982-June 1984—STEPS achieved an impressive placement rate of 61 percent. Equally impressive is the fact that nearly three-quarters of those placed were women, most of them single heads of households. Although terminated in 1984 due to lack of funding, the STEPS Program represents a sound model for effectively serving one of the hardest-to-employ populations.

Background

Denver's effort to train and place public assistance recipients evolved from the creative initiative of two city departments. The Department of Social Services, in conjunction with the Training and Employment Administration, developed the concept of "training force"—as opposed to workforce—in the belief that training AFDC clients for private sector employment was more cost effective than placing them in public service jobs. With the concurrence of the Colorado Department of Social Services, the STEPS Program was initiated in January 1982 as a local alternative to WIN's Community Work Experience Program.

Organizational Involvement and Funding

In addition to Denver's two city departments, the administration of STEPS involved linkages with two other service delivery entities. The Denver office of the state-run WIN program, which screened potential participants and made referrals, was one. The other service provider, to which client referrals for training were made, was the Denver Area Center for Employment Training (DACET). A local nonprofit organization with a strong track record in training and placing hard-to-employ individuals, DACET performed as a subcontractor to the city's Training and Employment Administration.

Funding for the STEPS Program in the amount of $243,000 came entirely from local property tax revenues. This "sole source" approach to funding—particularly where the source is local revenues—is quite rare among employment and training programs. It proved, in the end, to be the Achilles heel of STEPS, as the Program's funding was discontinued due to a lack of continued political support.

Characteristics of the Target Population

Ninety-six percent of participants in the STEPS Program were recipients of AFDC benefits. The characteristics of this group —much like those of AFDC beneficiaries elsewhere—were 73 percent female, almost all of whom were single heads of households; 97 percent under forty-five years of age; 39 percent Black; 17 percent Mexican-American; 16 percent White; 8 percent Spanish-American; 3 percent American Indian; and 1 percent Asian/Pacific Islanders. This racial/ethnic diversity among the Program's clients suggests the complexity of serving such a group, a group which also numbered 40 percent high school dropouts and of whom 100 percent were economically disadvantaged.

Key Elements

The basic philosophy of STEPS, according to Denver's Training and Employment Administrator, was that training followed by employment would be provided to interested and committed AFDC clients. In this regard, the program represented an alternative to mandatory workforce programs.

Training

The focus of STEPS training services was short term—four to six months—involving intensive skill and job-preparedness training. An open entry/open exit arrangement allowed participants a good measure of flexibility—important to many whose personal and family circumstances required such flexibility.

The curriculum for training was composed of three main elements: skills instruction, understanding employer expectations, and developing positive and strong work habits. To assist participants in meeting requirements of the curriculum, workshops were conducted regularly.

Selection of occupations to which training services were tailored was based on criteria of: (1) being in demand; (2) paying entry-level wages of $4.50 or more per hour; (3) offering full-time employment; and (4) offering opportunities for upward mobility. In addition, an emphasis was placed on non-traditional occupations into which women could enter at reasonable wages.

Among the occupations chosen for training through the STEPS Program were: electronic testing and assembly, electromechanical assembly, information processing, sheet metal fabrication, machine shop production, building maintenance and shipping and receiving.

Business Advisory Council

The Denver business community was integrally involved in the selection of occupations for training in two ways. First, business persons served on a local advisory council which oversaw program policies and procedures. Second, the line supervisors from local businesses monitored training activities to ensure their effectiveness and appropriateness to the private sector.

Results

Of the 190 individuals served through STEPS, 116 were placed in full-time private sector jobs—a 61 percent placement rate. The average wage for this group was $4.92 per hour, with men averaging $5.51 and women $4.69 per hour. As a result of being employed, STEPS participants—72 percent of whom were women—were able to end their dependence on welfare, become economically self-sufficient and, in doing so, reduce the cost to the public of providing public assistance.

Denver's initiative, though short-lived due to funding problems, offers a successful model for serving a typically difficult-to-serve population. The goal of the Program —to place AFDC recipients in in-demand occupations following short-term, intensive, yet flexible skills training—suggests much about what works for this population.

In contrast, the problems associated with using local tax revenues as the sole source of funding suggest what may, in fact, not work—at least for the long term.

For More Information Contact:

Betty Sparrow, Manager
Program Operations Division
Denver Employment and Training Administration
1440 Fox Street
Denver, CO 80204-2615
(303) 893-3382

JOB CREATION FOR UNSKILLED WORKERS
Linking Employment and Local Economic Development

THE SER LEARNING CENTER
San Antonio, Texas

Bottom-line solutions to the problems of urban unemployment lie in providing job opportunities for groups and individuals in need. The most effective—and arguably only—means of creating jobs in meaningful numbers is through planned, focused and coherent economic development initiatives. But even the best-planned, best-focused and most coherent initiatives will not yield jobs for workers in need unless those workers are prepared—with basic education and job-specific skills—to meet employers' needs.

In San Antonio, Texas, a city government project aimed at preparing unskilled adults for jobs created through economic development has served more than 2500 local residents. Focusing on English-as-a-Second-Language (ESL), Adult Basic Education (ABE) and Graduate Equivalent Degrees (GEDs), the SER Learning Center readies workers for on-the-job skill training and full-time employment opportunities. Placement of local residents in development-generated, entry-level positions is assured through "First Source" hiring agreements between the city and businesses receiving assistance.

Background

The SER Learning Center—originally the Fair Break Center—was established in 1980 in conjunction with a large-scale economic development project in downtown San Antonio. The project, entitled Vista Verde, represented a $100-million invest-

ment of public and private capital and encompassed 150 acres in one of the City's oldest and poorest areas. In partnership with the City Government was the U.S. Department of Housing and Urban Development, a California real estate developer and Control Data Corporation.

With an Urban Development Action Grant (UDAG) and infrastructure improvements as incentives, Vista Verde was able to attract a mix of high technology and service industries to San Antonio's center. The linchpin of the project was an electronic assembly plant, owned and operated by Control Data's subsidiary, Magnetic Peripherals, Inc.

As part of its UDAG agreement with the City, Control Data helped to establish an educational center designed to prepare low-income San Antonians for employment at the plant. To facilitate the education process, the company and the city jointly purchased a PLATO computer learning system, a self-paced instructional program.

Organizational Involvement and Funding

Originally a partnership between the city of San Antonio and Control Data Corporation, the Fair Break Center was established in 1980. In 1981, overall administration of the Center was contracted out to Project SER, a community-based nonprofit organization specializing in pre-employment training of disadvantaged San Antonians. At this time, the Fair Break Center became the SER

Learning Center. The screening and assessment component—considered a key to the Center's success—has been administered under subcontract by Goodwill Industries of San Antonio. In designing this component, Goodwill incorporated successful features of screening and assessment techniques from around the country.

Funding for the Center has declined over the last five years, having begun with $1.2 million in CETA funds in 1980. For Program Year 1985, the Center received $284,000 in JTPA Title II-A funds. Exploration of additional resources, including possible linkage with the Comprehensive Competencies Program, is a high priority of the Center's staff.

Characteristics of the Target Population

San Antonio's economically disadvantaged population is composed predominantly of Hispanic families and individuals, a characteristic reflected in the Center's participant mix. Eighty-seven percent of current participants are of Hispanic origin, 7 percent are Black, 5 percent are White and 1 percent is comprised of other groups. Approximately 60 percent of the clients are male, and all participants must be between the ages of eighteen and twenty-six and have a sixth grade education or less.

As a reflection of the size of the city's disadvantaged population, all participants must meet JTPA standards for being disadvantaged; there is no 10 percent "window."

Key Elements

Having originated as part of the Vista Verde development project, the SER Learning Center was designed to provide educa-tional and training services to would-be employees of Control Data's electronics assembly subsidiary. The approach to providing these services was to structure half-day classroom education sessions during which the self-paced PLATO computer learning system was utilized. The second half of each day was spent in on-the-job training of electronics assembly at the Magnetic Peripherals plant.

The development of an effective system of screening and assessment has been a major factor in the eventual success of the Center's participants. Developed by Goodwill Industries, the system "weeds out" applicants with barriers such as substance addiction and refers them to appropriate social service agencies for treatment and counseling. With the introduction of the Goodwill system, the placement rate of Center participants doubled from 40 to 80 percent.

Results

In the six years in which the Center has been in operation, a total of 2504 participants have graduated from one or more of the programs offered. The majority of this number have received either a Graduate Equivalent Degree (1277), an Adult Basic Education Certificate (851) or an English-as-a-Second-Language Certificate (376). A total of 2003 participants have gone on to enroll in job training programs, with 500 of this group having been placed in jobs, 150 of these at Magnetic Peripherals. As essentially an educational service provider, the SER Learning Center counts placements among individuals who enroll in job training programs as well as those who enter employment. The combined placement rate for Center graduates is a most impressive 80 percent.

For More Information, Contact:

Belvin Steward
Employment and Training Division
City of San Antonio
434 S. Main Street
Suite 301
San Antonio, Texas 78204
(512) 299-7011

LOCAL JOBS FOR LOCAL RESIDENTS
The "First Source" Approach

THE EMPLOYMENT AGREEMENTS PROGRAM
Portland, Oregon

As cities have long been the center of commerce and trade activity, they too have been the locus of employment for almost all but agricultural workers. With the advent of the automobile and highways to carry them, workers began living outside central cities, thus spawning the commuter phenomenon. And, while lower taxes, transportation ease and access to more space for single-story production facilities have attracted certain businesses to ex-urban areas, the fact remains that cities continue to provide large numbers of employment opportunities. The always-smoldering controversy is whether earning a paycheck downtown—and, in so doing, utilizing city services—and spending it in the suburbs constitutes an unfair drain on city resources. When the use of city resources for economic development assistance is at issue, the controversy over who should benefit from resultant job opportunities can be considerably hotter.

In basic terms, "First Source" employment agreements involve negotiated contracts between a city and a business receiving economic development assistance whereby local residents—often targeted segments of the community—are hired for jobs generated by that development. While the terms of agreements, their enforceability, and the types of jobs covered may vary, the underlying concept is one of local jobs for local residents.

Background

The city of Portland, Oregon has been a leader among cities in the use of employment agreements as a condition for acceptance of publicly-provided economic development assistance. In the seven years in which First Source agreements have been in use, more than 600 Portland residents have been hired by some twenty-five employers. The Employment Agreements Program (EAP) is targeted to economically disadvantaged Portlanders, many of whom are unskilled and lacking in basic education.

In Portland, in 1978, a study of labor force demographics revealed that the city was the workplace for more than half of the region's workers, while only 35 percent of those workers resided within the city. Negotiating with a major electronics firm at the time, the then-mayor of Portland sought to ensure that any development assistance to the firm should result in direct benefits—i.e., jobs—to Portland residents. Additional considerations for employing local residents were the relative lessening of air pollution from fewer commuters and less strain on the city's infrastructure. In 1979, the electronics firm, Wacker Siltronics, entered into Portland's first negotiated hiring agreement, an agreement which resulted in 444 jobs for local residents.

72

Organizational Involvement and Funding

The evolution of Portland's First Source Program, later renamed the Employment Agreements Program, involved several employment and economic development organizations. The Training and Employment Division of the City's Human Resources Bureau (which originally operated the program), the Portland Development Commission, the City Loan Corporation and the Portland Private Industry Council (which operates the EAP today) all worked in concert to create hiring programs for local residents. Until recently, all First Source agreements were subject to the approval of the Portland City Council or the County Commission.

In its early stages, the First Source Program received a $2 million discretionary grant and a $195,000 Targeted Jobs Demonstration Grant, both from the U.S. Department of Labor. The program also received CETA monies which, in recent years, have been replaced by JTPA funds. In 1984 the PIC was awarded a $10,000 JTPA Title II-A grant for staffing the EAP, the amount of which reflects the relatively low cost of administering the program.

Characteristics of the Target Population

Portland's Employment Agreements Program is targeted to the city's economically disadvantaged population. With an unemployment rate that climbed above 10 percent during the 1982 recession and continuing decline among the region's basic industries, the need for targeting job creation to the hardest-to-employ is paramount.

Characteristically, EAP participants have been approximately 60 percent White, 30 percent Black and 10 percent Hispanic, Asian and/or Native American. A little better than half of participants are male, about 15 percent receive some form of public assistance, and nearly 40 percent are high school dropouts.

Key Elements

First Source hiring agreements are negotiated on a company-by-company basis by staff of the Portland PIC. Following agreement on terms, the PIC recruits and screens prospective workers according to job requirements established by the company. A list of qualified, disadvantaged city residents is then developed, from which the employer selects potential hires. If no qualified applicants are available, the employer is free to hire a candidate of his own choosing with the stipulation that a good faith effort be made to hire city residents first. In cases were an impasse exists with respect to referred applicants, an arbitration process may be employed, however, no cases have reached arbitration to date.

The premier example of Portland's hiring agreements success, the Wacker Siltronics Company, points out the potential of First Source arrangements. In exchange for development assistance in the forms of tax advantages and land purchase terms, Wacker Siltronics hired 444 Portland Residents (out of a total 600 person workforce). Appropriate candidates from the city's disadvantaged population were recruited, screened and enrolled in a newly created Silicon Technology Training Program, a collaborative effort involving the city, Wacker Siltronics, Portland Community College and the Portland Opportunities Industrialization Center (OIC).

To facilitate training of the future Wacker employees, a "mini-plant" was custom-designed by Portland Community

73

College in which classroom instruction, work experience and on-site plant training were provided by instructors who had observed Wacker's West German operations. In addition to filling job slots identified in the hiring agreement, Wacker hired workers for other positions through the First Source Program.

Based on the success of the Wacker agreement, a plan was developed for a permanent First Source Program covering all development assistance packages provided by the city. Elements of the citywide strategy included targeting residents of certain neighborhoods for job creation, creating pre-agreement negotiations procedures and establishing arbitration provisions for settling disputes between the city and employers.

Results

The effectiveness of a "First Source" hiring agreements policy must first be measured against the level of economic development activity taking place within a city. Second, the feasibility of such a policy must be considered in light of: (a) the composition, needs and problems of potential populations, (b) the availability of resources and (c) the capacity of local institutions to prepare the disadvantaged and unskilled for employment. With respect to the first consideration, it is essential that hiring agreements be marketed as a "service to business" from which benefits of applicant screening, assessment and preparation for employment are derived.

The second and third considerations require that coordination of resources and organizations takes place to ensure that hiring agreements programs are indeed services to business.

In Portland, the recent successes of the Employment Agreements Program have been tempered by the limited amount of development activity taking place. However, agreements which have been reached since 1979 have yielded more than 600 jobs for residents, many of whom would doubtless have difficulty finding such jobs otherwise. The majority of Portland's new jobs have been in manufacturing, clerical and sales occupations, with the average wage for entry-level jobs being $4.50 per hour.

In marked contrast to the Urban Development Action Grant Program (in which only one in ten low-income individuals obtains a new job), Portland's EAP initiative assures that most, if not all, development-generated jobs are filled by the city's disadvantaged population. Of further encouragement is the fact that a 1983 study of Portland's agreements revealed high job retention rates and satisfaction with the program among employers.

For More Information, Contact:

Lisa Nisenfeld, Vice President
Gonzales and Nisenfeld
3322 N.W. 35th
Portland, OR 97210
(503) 295-0315

ASSISTING THE LONG-TERM UNEMPLOYED
Creative Applications of Local Resources

THE WORK OPPORTUNITIES PROGRAM
Minneapolis, Minnesota

Long-term unemployed adults represent one of the most problematic of all groups. In addition to being alienated from the traditional world of work, the abject poverty and array of personal problems besetting the long-term unemployed make efforts on their behalf extremely difficult and often only marginally effective.

Through the initiative of a local foundation and the combined efforts of its mayor and employment and training department, the city of Minneapolis created opportunities for jobs and training for approximately 650 long-term unemployed residents. The success of the Work Opportunities Program resulted in its use as a model for the Minnesota Emergency Employment Program (MEED), a statewide program for unemployed workers in crisis.

Background

In 1982, in the face of rising unemployment and increasing fiscal constraints on public funds, directors of the local McKnight Foundation approached the mayors of Minneapolis and St. Paul with a proposal to fund job creation efforts on behalf of the cities' long-term unemployed residents. The goal of the Foundation was to generate jobs as quickly as possible and, in so doing, provide much-needed income to individuals who averaged only $428 in earnings for the six-month period prior to enrollment in the program.

Organizational Involvement and Funding

The McKnight Foundation contributed a total of $1.175 million dollars to the funding of the Program's three main components. In addition, $250,000 in JTPA Title II-A funds was allocated through the Minneapolis Employment and Training Program, the agency responsible for developing and coordinating program components. A Minneapolis brokerage firm, Piper-Jaffray, Inc., had pledged $50,000 in incentive funds for a fourth program component involving private sector job creation. That program, however, was abandoned in favor of the other, more expeditious approaches to generating jobs.

Characteristics of The Target Population

Minneapolis' long-term unemployed population numbers 50-60,000 individuals, approximately 13-16 percent of the city's 370,000 total population. In order to target the very neediest among the long-term unemployed, individuals receiving AFDC or Unemployment Insurance were not eligible for the Work Opportunities Program. As a result, the average six-month income of participants prior to entering the program was $428.

A survey of 333 participants yielded the following demographic breakdown: 41 percent Whites, 41 percent Blacks, 9 percent Native Americans, 6 percent Asians and 1 percent Hispanics. Approximately two-thirds of clients were male, and a majority were between twenty and thirty. The educational levels of participants revealed some rather striking dimensions of Minneapolis' long-term unemployed, as 54 percent were high school graduates and nearly one-quarter (24 percent) had some education beyond high school. Only 22 percent of participants placed had less than a high school diploma.

Key Elements

A combination of community service employment, private sector on-the-job training and transitional part-time work provided a flexible response to addressing the individual needs of Minneapolis' long-term unemployed.

Community Service Employment
The "immediate response" component, Community Service Employment, provided much-needed money to individuals in return for a variety of useful community projects. In addition to the $4.00 - 4.25 per hour wages, the work experience led to private sector jobs for 22 percent of this group. Considering the multiple employment barriers affecting these individuals, this represents a rather creditable placement rate.

On-the-Job Training
The OJT component of the Work Opportunities Program created short-term private sector jobs and training opportunities. It did so by paying 100 percent of training wages for a two-month period, combining federal JTPA funds for the standard 50 percent and McKnight Foundation funds for the other 50 percent. Wages for OJT participants ranged from $4.50 to $5.00 an hour, and training was primarily in assembly work trades.

Transitional Part-time Work
This component was established to provide minimum wage, part-time employment to individuals enrolled in vocational education programs. The cost of wages was underwritten with JTPA Title II-A funds for adult training activities. On the average, participants in the vocational programs worked between eight and ten hours per week.

Results

In the approximately two-year period during which the Work Opportunities Program was in operation (1983-84), a total of 645 long-term unemployed Minneapolis residents were placed in employment or on-the-job training. A breakdown of the results of each program is as follows:

Community Service Employment— 250 individuals placed in six-month positions in the nonprofit sector. Fifty-five CSE participants transitioned into private sector employment following their service.

On-the-Job Training—Seventy-two of an original 93 trainees completed training and became unsubsidized employees, most performing various forms of assembly work.

Transitional Part-time Employment— Approximately 300 residents participated in this part-time program while enrolled in vocational education programs. In additions, ten jobs were created under the Job Creation Incentive Program which the City abandoned in lieu of the other, quicker job-generating programs.

As the model for the Minnesota Emergency Employment Program (MEED), Minneapolis' efforts on behalf of its long-term unemployed residents were praiseworthy for their innovation in combining public and private (foundation) funds in a flexible, multi-component structure. Through tight administration of the programs, the City kept administrative costs to approximately 5.5 percent of the overall WOP budget.

For More Information, Contact:

Chip Wells, Coordinator, Program Operations
Minneapolis Employment and Training Program
Room 310½
City Hall
Minneapolis, MN 55415
(612) 348-4386

EMPLOYING THE HOMELESS
Creative Approaches To A Complex Problem

THE HOMELESS PILOT JOB PROJECT/THE JOBS TRYOUT PROJECT
San Francisco, California

An often-complex array of personal, social and economic problems contribute to and, frequently, result in the human condition known as "homelessness." While commonalities exist in the roots of these problems—among them the attendant pressures of a mass society and an increasingly specialized, skill-dependent labor economy—the individuality of circumstances leading to homelessness creates an equally complex problem of how society should respond. Indeed, the willing choice of some individuals to live outside the mainstream makes any social response inappropriate, though the majority of the homeless population suffer from illness and/or hardships which are wholly involuntary.

Nowhere is the problem of homelessness more magnified and exacerbated than in cities. The reality of this problem, given its multiple dimensions, is that attempts to resolve it are only selectively applicable and less often effective. On the other hand, for many among the homeless, there exists the desire to regain stability and sufficiency within their lives. For these individuals, the opportunity to obtain employment offers the best, if not the only, prospect.

The city of San Francisco, through the initiative and leadership of its mayor, experimented with a two-phase project aimed at developing the employability of homeless adults. The first phase, the Homeless Pilot Jobs Project, placed one hundred participants in public service positions with various city agencies and departments; the second, the Jobs Tryout Project, used wage subsidies to pay employers in the private, nonprofit and public sectors to provide training to forty-three homeless individuals, with the expectation of hiring after successful completion of training. While the results, in terms of percentage of placements, terminations, etc., are not particularly telling, the projects are presented here for their approach to and instructive experience in addressing the employment problems of homeless adults.

Background

In recent years, dramatic increases in the size of San Francisco's homeless population—the number may be as high as 15,000—have heightened the concerns of city officials and human service providers for the needs and problems of this population. Among these concerns was the inability of most homeless people to earn even minimal incomes, largely a factor of not having worked steadily for many years, if ever. The lack of income from not working, in turn, contributed determinably to the unaffordability of housing, hence the condition of homelessness.

From concerns of the entire San Francisco community for its homeless residents came the formation, in 1983, of a Task Force on the Homeless by Mayor Diane Feinstein. Composed of representatives from city departments and local service providers, the Task Force met several times to address fundamental problems affecting this growing segment of the community. With respect to employment-related problems, the Task Force came up with a proposal for a two-phase project which is the subject of this case study: the Homeless Pilot Jobs Project/Jobs Tryout Project.

Organizational Involvement and Funding

With the Mayor's Task Force on the Homeless providing overall direction for both projects, decidedly different approaches were taken to the development of each. This distinction is reflected both in the organizations/entities involved and funding sources of the respective projects.

The Homeless Jobs Pilot Project

In this first phase, the Mayor's Office of Employment and Training, in conjunction with the Mayor's Office of Criminal Justice and ten local service providers, planned and designed the Pilot Project. Funding in the amount of $279,446 of general revenues was allocated by the Mayor's Office and approved by the Board of Supervisors. The Pilot Project was administered by the Mayor's Office of Employment and Training, with assessment and referral functions conducted by ten social service provider agencies (which acted as the point-of-contact with the homeless population).

The Jobs Tryout Project

In contrast to the multi-party involvement in the Pilot Project, the Jobs Tryout Project was the sole administrative responsibility of the San Francisco Private Industry Council. The city government's link to the project—aside from the Task Force oversight—came from the Community Development Block Grant Program which funded the Project in the amount of $191,600. In-kind contributions came from PIC resources.

Characteristics of The Target Population

As noted above, San Francisco's homeless population—the exact size of which is unknown—may number as high as 15,000. What is known is that the population has been increasing dramatically in recent years. Three factors, independently and unrelatedly, account for this increase.

First, deinstitutionalization of thousands of mentally ill persons has resulted in many of them becoming homeless. A measurement of this factor is that the number of state psychiatric hospital beds for severely mentally disturbed people in California declined from one bed for every 430 state residents in 1960 to one bed for every 4,800 residents—a more than 1,000 percent decrease. Second, as a result of urban renewal and the gentrification of many previously low-rent neighborhoods, the availability of low-income housing has been greatly reduced. Third, increases in structural unemployment, particularly in cities, have sent more and more individuals and families into poverty, while, at the same time, the migration of poor and near-poor people to cities has increased.

Statistics on and characteristics of San Francisco's homeless population, taken from monthly surveys, include the following:

■ 52 percent of the population are White, 28 percent are Black, Native Americans account for 3 percent and Hispanics 1 percent

- The medium age of the population is 31.4 years
- A third have lived in San Francisco for less than three months; 17 percent for less than a year
- 68 percent have marketable skills; 71 percent have held a job for more than one year
- 56 percent have completed high school; 17 percent are college graduates
- Potentially more than 40 percent suffer from mental illness; substance abuse may affect in excess of 60 percent.

Key Elements

The Homeless Jobs Pilot Project

The design of the Pilot Project called for one hundred jobs to be filled in public and nonprofit agencies. City departments, including Public Works, Housing, Parks and Recreation and the MUNI Railway, accounted for ninety of the one hundred slots, while the other ten were with community-based organizations which provide services to the homeless. These same provider organizations performed intake, screening and referral functions for all project participants.

Duties performed by the Pilot Project participants varied according to the department or agency in which they were placed, as well as the skill and ability levels of the individuals. Ninety-three of the one hundred were involved in cleanups projects, parks beautification, and general labor; these workers were paid $415/biweekly. The other seven participants were placed in clerical positions and received $407 biweekly.

The Jobs Tryout Project

Operated by the San Francisco Private Industry Council from October 1983 through August 1984, this second phase was essentially an on-the-job training initiative. Forty-three homeless individuals were placed with private, nonprofit and public employers, with wage subsidies—in the amount of $950 per month—paid to employers in return for providing on-the-job training. Employers were expected to hire the workers permanently if the tryout period proved successful. PIC staff provided counseling and follow-up services to monitor the progress of participants.

Results

San Francisco experiments with employment initiatives on behalf of homeless individuals offer instructive insight into working with one of the hardest-to-employ of all adult populations. The city's approach, including the designation of a "troubleshooter" in each participating city department, reflects the especial considerations associated with placing clients with multiple employment obstacles. Additionally, the commitment, on the part of the city's leaders, of city revenues and discretionary CDBG funds to a segment of the community without political clout is noteworthy.

As "pilot" and "tryout" projects, San Francisco's efforts to employ homeless people were modest in their bottom-line successes. Owing largely to the complex personal and health-related problems of participants—as well as to the transiency of homeless people in general—the Homeless Jobs Pilot Project placed only 17 percent of the total 132 participants. The PIC-operated Jobs Tryout Project achieved a 35 percent placement rate (15 placed out of 43 through its OJT approach).

Aside from the income and work experience which accrued to the individuals placed in jobs, the two projects resulted in valuable public service work having been performed within the community. The satisfaction of supervisors—to the surprise of some—with the quality of work and job performance of most participants attests to the quality of the work performed. The employer satisfaction also suggests that the barriers to employment facing the homeless are not insurmountable and, further, that mutual benefits can be realized from employing the homeless in public service capacities.

For communities considering employment initiatives on behalf of homeless residents, drawing on San Francisco's experience offers both insight into positive characteristics and a model upon which improvements can be based. One aspect of the projects which offers both is the role of service provider agencies in a partnership approach. On the positive side, the provider agencies function as an identifiable point of contact with the target population and, as such, are in the best position to screen, assess and refer clients for participation. On the negative side, only one of the ten providers involved in the projects offered counseling and support services to participants once referral was made. Considering the special problems and needs of the homeless population and the unique position of providers to address them, an ongoing counseling and support function appears critical to reducing turnover of project participants.

For More Information, Contact:

Brenda Brown
Chief of Special Projects
San Francisco Private Industry Council
1748 Market Street
San Francisco, California 94103
(415) 621-6853

PUBLIC SERVICE EMPLOYMENT FOR DISADVANTAGED ADULTS

THE MAYOR'S ON-THE-JOB TRAINING PROGRAM
Tampa, Florida

With the replacement of the Comprehensive Employment and Training Act (CETA) by the Job Training Partnership Act (JTPA) in 1982, the single biggest change to occur was the termination of federally-funded public service employment (PSE). Local governments across the country had utilized PSE slots to augment municipal department staffs, create innovative service delivery mechanisms and, in some instances, to hold down labor costs to local taxpayers. While the merits—and indeed the very concept—of public service employment continue to be sources of controversy and debate within public policy circles, the fact remains that PSE opportunities provided job training and work experience for many economically disadvantaged individuals. In addition, the targeting of PSE slots to segments of the community most in need, i.e., women, minorities, etc., contributed measurably to municipalities' attainment of equal employment opportunity goals.

Since April of 1983, the city of Tampa, Florida has operated its own version of a public service employment program, more aptly termed a municipal government employment and training initiative. The Mayor's On-The-Job Training Program, which is targeted to disadvantaged Tampa residents, has trained and placed 80 individuals—mostly women and minorities—in full-time municipal jobs in its first two years. The Mayor's Office estimates that 10 percent of all entry-level positions are filled in this way. With more than 80 percent of its funding derived from the city's general revenues, the Program is distinctly different from the CETA PSE component, while accomplishing many of the same objectives. The Program also helps to meet the city's equal employment opportunity goals.

Background

A local government initiative in the purest sense, the Mayor's OJT Program was the brainchild of Tampa Mayor Bob Martinez. The Mayor's commitment to creating equality of opportunity in municipal employment led to a comprehensive review of the hiring patterns and practices of every city department. Results of the study were used to ascertain whether municipal workforce characteristics reflected underemployment of women and minorities in certain departments or positions. The city's findings led to the creation of the Program, established with two specific goals: (1) to provide job training and placement in municipal positions for economically disadvantaged residents, and (2) to help the city government meet its staffing needs and EEO goals.

Organizational Involvement and Funding

Three city departments and the Tampa Private Industry Council cooperatively operate the Mayor's OJT Program. In addition to the Mayor's office itself, the Tampa Division of Urban Development and Job Training and the Department of Administration, within which rests the city's EEO function, comprise the local government involvement. The Tampa PIC is responsible for recruitment and screening of applicants, as well as supervision of trainees during the first of three phases of the training sequence.

As noted above, the major portion of the Program's resources come from the city's general revenues. The PIC supplies funding for the component of the Program for which it is responsible. For fiscal year 1985, the Mayor's OJT Program has allocated $168,000 in city funds and $40,000 in PIC funds.

Characteristics of the Target Population

Tampa's disadvantaged population reflects characteristics of similarly situated individuals elsewhere. Most have had less than a high school education and many lack basic educational skills. A lack of work experience and job-specific skills is also characteristic of the group.

A breakdown of participants in the Mayor's OJT Program reveals that 78 percent are Black, 11 percent are White and 11 percent are of Hispanic origin. On the average, participants have eleven years of education and little experience in jobs.

Key Elements

There are three phases to the Tampa Mayor's OJT Program. The first phase, which is four weeks in length, is a tryout period for candidates to explore the position and for supervisors to assess the candidate's potential. As part of its recruitment and screening function, the staff of the PIC oversees this phase of the Program.

The second phase of training involves actual performance in the position. Trainees are paid 90 percent of the position's starting salary during this phase. The length of training for this most important phase is variable dependent upon both the nature of the position and the rate at which the trainee grasps the essential functions and responsibilities.

The final phase of the Program is placement in the position on a full-time basis and at regular pay. It should be noted that all program participants who successfully complete training are guaranteed placement in a position with the city government.

The overall length of the training is variable according to the factors noted above. As a benchmark for each position's length of training, the city uses the U.S. Department of Labor Dictionary of Occupational Titles. The range of time is usually between six and twenty-six weeks, with flexibility built in to allow individuals to complete training early and begin regular employment. In the beginning stages of the Program, training for all positions lasted six months, however, the entry-level status of most jobs permitted modifying this rule for shorter durations.

Results

In its two years of operations, the Mayor's OJT Program has placed 80 disadvantaged Tampa residents in municipal jobs. Of the total 118 participants, this number represents a 68 percent placement rate. The other 38 participants either quit or were dropped from the program for chronic tardiness or unexcused absences. Currently there are 15 candidates undergoing training.

Trainees have been placed in a wide variety of local government positions, among them word processor operators, personnel technician, clerk-typist, police communications technician, heavy equipment operator, environmental sanitation inspector and wastewater facilities operator. The potential for trainees to be placed in other municipal jobs is quite good, since all city departments are required to participate in the Program.

The success of the Tampa Mayor's initiative is beginning to show signs of re-creating itself in the city's private sector. One large firm is currently replicating the city's approach, and the hope is that as many as ten or fifteen other local employers will follow suit. To encourage private sector initiatives of this kind, the city has developed an audio-visual presentation on the program for company executives and personnel directors.

For Further Information, Contact:

Roy Opfer, Division Manager
Tampa Division of Urban Development and
    Job Training
404 E. Jackson Street
Tampa, Florida 33602
(813) 223-8256

Chapter 5

DISLOCATED WORKERS
Opportunities For a New Beginning

DISLOCATED WORKERS
Opportunities For a New Beginning

The underlying causes of worker dislocation in the United States are technological change within the workplace, competition with/from off-shore and foreign-produced goods and an economy in transition from a manufacturing to a service base. Manifestations of the problem are most recognizable in workforce reductions, mass lay-offs and plant closings. Fundamentally, though, dislocation is a human problem, affecting the lives of workers, their families and, in some cases, entire communities.

Efforts to address economic dislocation most often focus on the personal and professional needs of dislocated workers as individuals. Other efforts address groups of workers displaced, typically, from the same source of employment at the same time. Still others attempt to address the problem prior to workers' separation from their jobs.

The six case studies in this chapter reflect these variations in approach to the problems of dislocated workers. They also represent distinctions in local, regional and industry-specific approaches, as well as differences in sources of leadership and scale of effort. Common to a000035the involvement of more than a single entity, with most involving combinations of several.

Buffalo, New York is the subject of the first case, in which the city and its county provide comprehensive training and re-employment services to victims of plant closings and the general decline of the area's economic base. A JTPA Title III program with funding from other sources as well, the Buffalo and Erie County Worker Reemployment Program stresses the initiative of the worker in becoming reemployed, with program resources considered the tools to support the worker's initiative.

Another full-service effort to re-employ dislocated workers is the approach of St. Louis, Missouri's Metropolitan Re-employment Project (MRP). Long and active involvement on the part of a key area business group and coordination of services by the St. Louis Community College are the hallmarks of this initiative. The MRP addresses the needs of workers individually, as well as in employer-specific groups, and attempts, where possible, to intervene before layoffs or closings occur.

Anticipation of plant closings and large-scale layoffs offers the best prospect for ameliorating dislocation. In Fort Wayne, Indiana, advance planning and close co-operation between a major employer and organized labor resulted in 4,000 workers being reemployed in a three-year period. The centerpiece of the Fort Wayne initiative was an outplacement center which today remains a model for dislocated worker reemployment.

A local government initiative which later evolved into a state center for dislocated workers was Des Moines, Iowa's response to a dislocated worker crisis. Faced with the shutdown of two companies and the prospects of several others closing, local officials formed a task force of companies, unions and the Private Industry Council which developed a multi-dimensional strategy to help workers find new jobs. Assistance was also provided to area farmers who experienced economic distress.

Another model of local leadership comes from the city-county of Butte-Silver Bow, Montana. In this case, decline of the area's copper mining industry forced more than 2,700 workers out of jobs, and retraining offered the only hope for finding new ones. The Chief Executive of the city-county government enlisted the help and resources of industry, labor, and all levels of government to create three worker retraining/reemployment programs, all of which have been highly successful.

The last of the Dislocated Worker case studies profiles the efforts of two Oregon cities and their surrounding county to address the needs of dislocated timber industry workers. Eugene and Springfield, Oregon, in cooperation with Lane County Community College, merged their JTPA service delivery areas to couple resources for assisting and retraining workers. In its first year, the Lane Community College Dislocated Worker Program placed 87 percent of the clients it served.

COMPREHENSIVE SERVICES AND WORKER INITIATIVE
Solutions To Large-Scale Dislocation

THE WORKER REEMPLOYMENT PROGRAM
Buffalo and Erie County, New York

Since 1982, the Worker Reemployment Program (WRP) has been an integral part of the Buffalo area's efforts to stabilize unemployment in an economy wracked by severe losses in the manufacturing sector. Operated by the Private Industry Council for Buffalo and Erie County, the program is a two-tiered approach to the problems of dislocation, targeting both specific plant closings/layoffs and job losses in the general economy. A comprehensive range of services—including outreach, assessment, classroom skill training, on-the-job training, self-directed job search and placement—support the program's philosophic approach of providing dislocated workers with the necessary tools to find and acquire new jobs.

Background

In recent years, unemployment in the Buffalo area has exceeded the national average by approximately 40 percent. During the recession of 1982, the jobless rate peaked at 14 percent. It hovers, in 1985, around 10 percent.

Contributing measurably to Buffalo's high levels of unemployment is the loss of jobs—40,000 alone between 1979 and 1982—in the durable goods manufacturing sector. The total of non-manufacturing jobs declined as well, despite increases in service industries such as finance, insurance and real estate. In terms of plant closings, the Erie County Industrial Devel-

opment Agency counted 101 between 1969 and 1981, affecting more than 21,000 workers directly and an estimated 12,000 others indirectly. The current estimate of dislocated workers in the Buffalo area stands at 37,000.

Considering the size of the area's dislocated worker population, the continuing erosion of its industrial base, and a comparative difficulty in attracting new types of industries, Buffalo and Erie County face an enormous challenge to apply resources and energies as effectively as possible. For the workers themselves, the problem of finding and acquiring new jobs is compounded by the fact that, on average, available jobs will pay substantially less than those from which they were displaced.

Organizational Involvement and Funding

The Worker Reemployment Program is operated by the Buffalo and Erie County Private Industry Council (PIC). As both the administrative entity and grant recipient for the Buffalo-Cheektowaga-Tonawanda Consortium SDA, the PIC has a well-developed set of contractual and working relationships with employment and training organizations, economic development agencies and employers. The results of these relationships are reflected in the fact that over 2,000 employers have entered into OJT contracts with the PIC since 1979. The PIC is also responsible for the development of hiring plans for Urban Development Action Grants (UDAGs). Local government support for the Worker Reemployment Program is strong in each of the three SDA Consortium communities.

Initial funding for the Program was provided by the U.S. Department of Labor as one of six dislocated worker demonstration programs funded during 1982-83. In the second year, following a six-month delay due to local conflict over configuration of the SDA, the Program continued with funding from two sources: state-administered JTPA Title III funds—distributed on a formula basis, and a New York State-financed initiative to aid counties with significant dislocated worker populations, entitled the Emergency Employment Intervention Program Act (EEIPA).

During the program year which ended on June 30, 1985, the Worker Reemployment Program received $800,000 in JTPA funds and $2,200,000 from the EEIPA. Funding for the Program for the year beginning July 1, 1985, will come from a U.S. Department of Labor Title III Discretionary Grant for the Western New York area. (The EEIPA has been terminated, and Title III formula funds will be restricted to supporting OJT activities only.)

Characteristics of the Target Population

Numbering approximately 37,000, the most prominent and telling characteristic of the Buffalo area's dislocated worker population is its size. As noted above, the majority of this population were formerly employed in the seriously depressed durable goods manufacturing sector. The profiles of these workers can be described, in general, as "typical" of dislocated workers elsewhere: most likely over age 22, White, high school-educated or better, married with children, homeowners and veterans.

In its first year of operation, 1982, the Worker Reemployment Program served dislocated workers mainly from the area's declining steel industry, with 70 percent of its clients drawn from nine targeted plants. In year two, 1983, changes in targeting strategy resulted in 65 percent of clients having come from eighteen targeted plants, while the other 35 percent came from 300 different companies of all types. While changes in the targeting strategy did not require changes in the Program's service mix, significant changes in the characteristics of the client population were found, with second-year clients being, on average, younger, with less experience and lower wage levels, and less likely to be homeowners or heads of families.

For 1985, the Worker Reemployment Program has targeted an estimated 6,300 dislocated workers from thirty plants for reemployment assistance. Changes in client characteristics which resulted from targeting changes in previous years suggest the need for adaptability within the Program to service differing needs. On the bright side, the presence of younger workers within the client population suggests that there may be more flexibility in meeting their reemployment needs.

Key Elements

In a single word, the Buffalo and Erie County Worker Reemployment Program can be described as "comprehensive." The programmatic resources and staff expertise of the Private Industry Council combine to offer a broad range of service and assistance options to the area's dislocated worker population. These service and assistance options are viewed by the PIC staff as the essential "tools" to enable dislocated workers to gain new employment.

Self-Directed Job Search
At the heart of the Program is a method of self-directed job search, the underlying philosophy of which is that "looking for work is a full-time job." While the full range of training and related services are available to workers in need of them, heavy emphasis is placed on the worker taking the initiative to find and acquire a new job.

Outreach
To assist the reemployment efforts of dislocated workers at the earliest possible point, the Worker Reemployment Program performs an outreach function by working with management and union representatives from targeted companies in the process of laying off workers or closing down operations. The Program is explained, information is gathered—including layoff lists—and impacted workers are then contacted by letter. In order to reach workers already out of work or in non-targeted companies, Program staff coordinate efforts with the New York State Job Service, the United Way Hotline for the Unemployed, local Job Training Intake Sites and the local news media.

Orientation
Contacted workers are encouraged to attend group orientation sessions, held in community centers, union halls or the Reemployment Program's Center. Orientations cover Program and other available services, problems associated with finding a new job, and the importance of individual initiative. Presentations are made by dislocated workers themselves to lend credibility to the Program.

The Client Ability Profile
Following the orientation sessions, eligible and interested clients participate in a two-hour counseling session in which the job search approach is explained in further detail. Interviews, education and work histories and written test results are then combined to formulate a Client Ability Profile, used by the worker and job counselor to develop realistic employment goals and an appropriate services plan.

Intensive Job Search Workshop
An intensive four-day workshop to train dislocated workers in all aspects of self-directed job search is the next step. Upon completion of the workshop, participants work individually with a job counselor to match his or her Client Ability Profile with both general and specific job possibilities and to ascertain the need for other Program services.

Training Opportunities
Occupational Skills Training is available through local schools or the WRP Center for clients lacking experience and/or education in in-demand occupations. Employers must be involved in the development of training curricula and hiring agreements for successful completers must be secured. Performance-based contracting is used whenever possible, and training must be directed to in-demand occupations.

On-the-Job Training opportunities are available for clients who are generally prepared for work but who lack the necessary skills for a specific job. OJT-certified clients are encouraged to seek out jobs with employers, using the certificate as a leveraging tool. The Program staff feel that this approach contributes to a stronger commitment on the part of both employer and trainee than would be the case with an intermediary.

Job Search and Placement Assistance

Dislocated workers requiring only job search assistance—but assistance beyond what is offered through the intensive workshop—have available to them the Resource and Placement Center. This Center offers the use of telephones, newspapers, business directories, and typing and photocopying services.

The Program also employs a Vocational Information Processing System, a computerized system which provides quick, thorough and dependable information linking participants with available job opportunities. This system is a key to the overall placement success of the Worker Reemployment Program.

Supportive Services

Participants may receive up to $600 for out-of-town interviews and another $600 for relocation costs. Other supportive services, such as needs-based payments and child care, are available to eligible clients, and information on other sources of services is also provided.

Results

In its first year of operation, the Worker Reemployment Program placed 523 clients in jobs paying an average of $6.25 per hour. This number represented a placement rate of 65.5 percent of the 798 total Program participants. The placement rate for clients who received Job Search Assistance and On-the-Job Training was 67 percent; for those who received Job Search Assistance only, the rate was 62.4 percent; for OJT only, 75.8 percent; and for Occupational Skills Training, 57 percent. The cost of the Program per participant was $1,975. The cost per placement was $3,014, an amount 25 percent below the projected cost. Conversely, the placement percentage exceeded expectations.

In Program Year 1984, 7,000 outreach letters were sent to Buffalo area dislocated workers, to which 1,950 responses were received. Of these respondents, 1,350 signed up for orientation sessions, which in turn led to 877 enrollments in the Program. The expectations of Program staff is that 650 of these enrollees will be placed in jobs by September 1, 1985, representing a 76.5 percent placement rate.

For More Information, Contact:

Harry Reeverts, Program Director
Worker Reemployment Program
Buffalo and Erie County Private Industry
   Council, Inc.
699 Main Street
Buffalo, New York 14203
(716) 845-6830

A FULL-SERVICE APPROACH TO WORKER DISLOCATION

THE METROPOLITAN REEMPLOYMENT PROJECT
St. Louis, Missouri

As it operates today, the Metropolitan Reemployment Project (MRP) represents the evolution of a full-service approach to the problems and needs of dislocated workers in the St. Louis Metropolitan Area. Having begun, in 1981, as a jobs club program in conjunction with area unions, this partnership effort involving business, labor, government and education today provides a range of assessment, counseling, retraining and placement services, as well as planning and early intervention assistance in response to plant closings and layoffs. At the heart of the Project is an effective mix of committed organizations which share St. Louis' long-standing "spirit" of community cooperation.

Background

A city rich in its history of manufacturing and industrial accomplishments, St. Louis —like many others in the Midwest and Northeast—has been severely impacted by geographic and structural shifts in the nation's economy. The magnitude of this impact is suggested by the loss of more than 50,000 manufacturing jobs between 1979 and 1983. And while the metropolitan area's unemployment rate is today approximately the same as the national average—7 percent—the joblessness and reemployment problems of workers in "mature," i.e., declining, industries constitute pockets of much higher unemployment.

For communities in the St. Louis area, and for the workers who reside in them, the forces of economic transition—defined here as the decline of older industries and the emergence of newer ones—have presented problems as well as opportunities. Recognizing the presence of both, community leaders initiated an ambitious effort in the late 1970's to revitalize the area's economy. The Metropolitan Reemployment Project evolved as part of that effort.

Central to this evolution were the efforts of the New Spirit of St. Louis Labor/Management Committee, established in 1979 under the auspices of the Regional Commerce and Growth Association (RCGA). The "New Spirit" Committee, whose general purpose was to facilitate better labor-management relations within the area, identified plant closing and large-scale layoffs as one of the St. Louis area's most severe problems. The RCGA, which staffs the St. Louis Area Private Industry Council, in turn proposed the creation of the MRP.

Organizational Involvement and Funding

Since 1981, the MRP has been operated by and through the St. Louis Community College. A task force on unemployment, composed of representatives from labor, business, education and nonprofit organizations, serves as the board of directors for the Project with policy and oversight responsibilities. The Project maintains collaborative relationships with local government units within the metropolitan area,

93

particularly with economic development agencies.

Originally a pilot project under CETA, the MRP was primarily funded in 1982 and 1983 by an organization called Civic Progress, Inc. made up of the chief executive officers of major St. Louis companies. While training programs are now largely funded under JTPA through the Regional Commerce and Growth Association, Civic Progress continues to be the principal source of administrative funding. Additional support for retraining programs is provided by The Fund for the Improvement of Post-Secondary Education, and cash and in-kind support are derived from the St. Louis Community College, the Missouri Department of Employment Security, the RCGA and local businesses. Principal funding for the 1984 program year included:

$1,000,000 – JTPA Title III
   150,000 – Civic Progress
   100,000 – FIPSE
   175,000 – St. Louis Comm. Coll. (in-kind)
───────────
$1,425,000

Characteristics of the Target Population

The Metropolitan Reemployment Project targets displaced and laid off workers in the nine counties of Missouri and Illinois which comprise the St. Louis Metropolitan Area. Typically, these workers have stable work histories of several years, often with a single employer. The composition of MRP participants in the 1984 Program Year was 60 percent male, 63 percent White, 85 percent thirty years of age or older, and 50 percent with high school diplomas or better. Shifts in the composition of partici-

pants have produced increases in the percentage of Whites and college graduates, owing largely to the displacement of office and white collar workers due to automation. At the same time, however, the need for remedial education on the part of program participants also increased.

Key Elements

In contrast to many dislocated worker programs, the Metropolitan Reemployment Project is areawide in its focus and does not target specific closings. As the project has expanded its range of services, however, involvement in early responses to particular plant closings has taken place. The absence of an industry-specific focus has resulted in services being provided to workers from a wide variety of companies, including, as noted above, white collar workers from non-manufacturing businesses. The major components of the MRP service mix are:

Outreach

Information about the Project is communicated via unions, companies, social service agencies and public service announcements. As the Project has demonstrated success in reemploying workers, word-of-mouth communication has become an effective and credible recruitment means.

Job Shops/Conferences

Many MRP participants initially attend an intensive, one-day job shop in which basic information on searching for employment and obtaining social services is provided through various media and one-to-one counseling. The job shops are held at the Community College, in union halls and on company premises. Complementing these small group meetings are one-day conferences for up to 500 workers which cover ways of coping with personal, family and financial problems which beset the typical dislocated worker.

Outplacement Counseling
Experienced counselors work with Project participants through the reemployment process, providing skill assessments, general employment advice and specific job leads, as well as help with emotional and personal problems.

Job Clubs
Initiated in 1981, the job clubs were originally the main service feature of the MRP and were coordinated through union organizations. Beginning in 1983, the concept broadened to include on-site activities which begin with the announcement of an impending layoff or closing, thus facilitating retraining planning before the layoff actually occurs. Representatives from the MRP task force on unemployment work with company officials to arrange for on-site service programs.

Retraining Services
With JTPA resources, the Project provides on-the-job training to dislocated workers who exhibit basic skill adaptability. For those workers who require basic skill instruction, modest skills training programs are offered, as well as referral to other sources of retraining and assistance in planning group training programs. A special program, called the Experienced Workers Retraining Program and funded by the The Fund for the Improvement of Post-Secondary Education, has, since 1982, offered training in the fields of Business Services with Computer Applications and Electronics Technology.

An additional feature of the MRP is training services provided to the staffs of other agencies for establishing and operating dislocated worker programs.

Results

Since 1981, nearly 6,500 dislocated workers have been served by the Metropolitan Reemployment Project's programs. For one-third of these workers, successful reemployment can be documented; the actual number is believed to be significantly higher.

In the last program year for which complete data is available, 1983, the Project served 2,200 persons, nearly 650 of whom were placed in jobs. Of these, 186 received retraining, 201 had on-the-job training and 124 participated in job clubs.

For More Information, Contact:

Michael H. Maguire, Director
Metropolitan Reemployment Project
5600 Oakland Avenue
St. Louis, Missouri 63110
(314) 644-9142

ANTICIPATING A PLANT CLOSING
Business-Labor Cooperation for
Worker Outplacement

THE INTERNATIONAL HARVESTER/ UNITED AUTO WORKERS OUTPLACEMENT CENTER
Fort Wayne, Indiana

The closing of a major local business can have devastating effects on its workers and on the community in which they reside. Consensus among economic adjustment and dislocated worker experts is that the optimal strategy for dealing with plant closings/layoffs is one which begins prior to the actual occurrence.

In Fort Wayne, Indiana, the cooperative efforts of a major auto-related company and its labor organization helped to create a worker outplacement center to deal with the anticipated effects of the company shutdown. From its establishment in October 1982 to its closing in January 1985, the Center served 4,000 members of a 7,000-member dislocated total worker population. The concept and approach of the Fort Wayne initiative remain remarkable models for outplacement planning and reemployment.

Background

Sixty years after beginning operations in Fort Wayne, the International Harvester Corporation closed its doors in 1983. Having employed generations of Fort Wayne area residents in the production of farming and automotive machinery, the impact of the IH closing resounded throughout the community. The 7,000 workers displaced by the shutdown made up a large share of the area's 13 percent unemployment rate.

The economic crisis brought on by the IH closing came one year after Fort Wayne had experienced disaster of another nature —a major flood. In responding to the direct needs of their neighbors, 35,000 Fort Wayne residents volunteered to line riverbanks with a million sandbags and help evacuate families and businesses in distress. That spirit of community cooperation led to the first local assistance office ever established in a federal disaster center. It was a spirit that would again be tested in 1983, this time in response to the dislocation of large numbers of Fort Wayne workers. The outcome in this case was similarly remarkable.

The community's cooperative spirit and its effects were recognized as important contributors to Fort Wayne's designations in 1983, as an All-American City and as Most Livable City by the U.S. Conference of Mayors. As a means of continuing its progress, Mayor Winfield Moses oversees an aggressive economic development program and various public improvement projects. Strong support has been lent to these efforts by the Fort Wayne Chamber of Commerce.

Organizational Involvement and Funding

The Fort Wayne Outplacement Center was a cooperative effort involving International Harvester and the United Auto Workers, with IH principally managing the Center and the UAW handling recruitment, conducting workshops and identifying reemployment opportunities. Staffing of the Center was shared by members of the plant's workforce at all levels. The initiative did receive the strong support of local public officials, albeit through ancillary roles.

Initial funding for the Outplacement Center in 1983 was $380,000, established through negotiations with the UAW in 1982. Two hundred and fifty thousand dollars of this amount was used to reimburse workers for job-related course tuition. For 1984, the Center's second and last year in operation, $612,250 was awarded in JTPA Title III funds.

Characteristics of the Target Population

The International Harvester/United Auto Workers Outplacement Center was established to target reemployment services to the 7,000 workers dislocated by the IH plant closing. The characteristics of these workers were typical of auto industry workers elsewhere: family heads with stable work histories, skills limited to those used in their IH job, and little, if any, knowledge of how to locate new employment opportunities. In some cases, fathers and grandfathers of the permanent layoff victims had worked for IH, making the separation from the job that much more difficult.

Key Elements

Initiated prior to the plant's shutdown, the Outplacement Center focused on assisting the job search and reemployment efforts of the IH workforce. The key elements of the Center's service approach were:

Outplacement Workshops

Planned for groups of 20 workers, a set of two four-hour workshops addressed the range of problems confronting the laid-off or soon to be laid-off workers. Sessions covered personal and financial aspects of dislocation, as well as the obstacles of finding new jobs. Application procedures, interviewing technique and assessment of the state employment service network for job leads were all parts of the hands-on workshops.

Individual Job Search Counseling

This service was available from the Outplacement Center, together with job resource help, secretarial services for letters and resumes, and free use of long-distance telephone lines. Reference materials on alternative occupations and information on available training and employment opportunities nationwide were also provided.

Job Clubs

Regular meetings in groups of ten to twelve persons provided workers with an exchange of ideas, experiences and feelings concerning the job-search process. Job club participants also worked at contacting other IH workers who were not aware of or had not used the Center's services.

Job Development and Education Counseling

Beginning in the Center's second year of operations, job developers and education counselors were hired to assist workers in assessing the skills and aptitudes and to help match them with available training and reemployment opportunities.

Training

The IH/UAW Outplacement Center did not conduct any training programs itself. It did, however, facilitate workers' efforts to identify training opportunities elsewhere, including courses available through local institutions for IH reimbursed participants up to $1,000 if the courses were job-related. JTPA funds assisted other types of training, including OJT, which was utilized on a limited basis.

Results

The team approach of the Fort Wayne dislocated worker initiative was a major factor in the Center's serving 4,000 laid off workers. Of this number, 1,400 workers were placed in new jobs by the end of 1984. An additional 500 workers found jobs with International Harvester in other locations. Many other participants in the Outplacement Center's programs benefited from enhanced job search skills and have since found new employment.

The Fort Wayne initiative today remains a model for communities throughout the nation of successful business-labor cooperation. As inevitable changes in the structure of the economy continue, and with them come more complex problems of worker dislocation, the need for effective partnerships of employer and labor organizations will also continue.

The successful reemployment of Fort Wayne's dislocated worker population has been aided by a rather remarkable recovery in the area's economy. Since 1983, eighty-five new manufacturing concerns have opened in the area, the most significant one being a General Motors high-tech truck assembly plant which, when fully operative, will employ 3,000 workers.

For More Information, Contact:

Cletus Edmond, Director, Labor Relations
City of Fort Wayne
City-County Building, Rm. 330
Fort Wayne, IN
(219) 427-1180

RESPONDING TO CRISIS

A COMMUNITYWIDE INITIATIVE
FOR REEMPLOYMENT
Des Moines, Iowa

The shutdown of two major employers in 1981 and predictions of several other shutdowns produced a crisis in the Des Moines area, a crisis affecting thousands of workers in manufacturing industries. Des Moines' response to the crisis, initiated by the city government at the request of the region's Federation of Labor, the Private Industry Council and the impacted companies, resulted in the formation of a local task force and the establishment of a displaced worker transition center that same year. The success of this local initiative— aside from the more than 900 workers who have received reemployment assistance— is suggested by its evolution and expansion into the State of Iowa's Region XI Dislocated Worker Center. The area's dislocated farmers were also served by the center.

Background

The potential for the dislocation of 4,000 workers provided the impetus for the Des Moines community effort. Closing of the farm equipment manufacturer, Massey Ferguson, and Wilson Foods Company had already occurred in mid-1981; a similar fate seemed imminent for other businesses as well. The seriousness of this crisis was heightened by the fact that Des Moines' local economy had been historically strong and stable.

A truly communitywide effort was launched by Mayor Peter Crivara with the formation of the Task Force on Plant Closing and Retraining. Comprised of more than fifty leaders from business, labor,

education, government and community organizations, the Task Force set an ambitious agenda of assessing the impact of the closings and developing and implementing retraining programs. In addition to targeting reemployment assistance to workers in manufacturing industries, the Task Force also focused on the problems of dislocated farmers.

To carry out its agenda, the Des Moines Task Force formed five committees, one of them focusing specifically on the Massey Ferguson and Wilson closings. A second committee set its work on developing the concept of the worker transition center, while a third was responsible for promotional materials. The fourth and fifth committees, respectively, were charged with identifying job opportunities in in-demand occupations and developing training programs tailored to those occupations.

Organizational Involvement and Funding

As with any plant closing or major layoff, the deepest interests lie within the workers impacted and the companies experiencing decline. The case of Des Moines, Iowa, is no exception. Initial impetus to what would become a communitywide effort came from the South Central Iowa Federation of Labor and officials from Massey Ferguson and Wilson Foods. Together with the Central Iowa Private Industry Council, labor and business representatives approached Mayor Crivara about taking the lead in organizing a community response.

In initially establishing the Task Force

on Plant Closing and Retraining, and in lending continued support and participation, the role of the chief elected official has been an important factor in developing and maintaining consensus and momentum for this effort.

The cornerstone of the Des Moines initiative is the Displaced Worker Transition Center, today known as the Dislocated Worker Center.

During the 1984 program year, the Center was funded with $451,130 of state JTPA Title III funds. The Title III requirement of 35 percent matching funds was met with in-kind contributions of space and staff time for intake by the state Job Service, with United Way staff time—the Center is managed by the Labor Department of the United Way of Central Iowa—and with free medical service from the University of Osteopathic Medicine and Health Services.

Characteristics of the Target Population

As noted above, the Des Moines initiative targeted both manufacturing workers and dislocated farmers, reflecting the diversity of the area's economic base. The majority of the target population—mid-to late-thirties in age, White and male—was, however, employed in manufacturing. Most had worked steadily for at least ten years, and many for only one employer. Having had a single job in a now declining manufacturing economy, the challenge to workers to find new opportunities—most of them in the service sector—was quite formidable.

Key Elements

The Iowa Region XI Dislocated Worker Center—successor to original local initiative—offers a range of programs and services aimed at reemploying workers. While components of the Center's operations are typical of other dislocated worker initiatives, the mix of resources and efforts provides a good model for a communitywide effort. Important features of the Des Moines Center are:

Outreach
A variety of informational channels are used to reach workers and farmers, including written materials, public service announcements, business and labor spokespersons and referrals by social service agencies.

Assessment
Center staff determine participant eligibility for assistance according to JTPA criteria. Initial screening is performed to determine precise assistance needs; participants determined not to need retraining are given workshops—totalling twenty hours—on job search skills.

Job Development
In conjunction with the state Employment Service, the Task Force committees on job development pursue existing job opportunities and identify occupations with near-term growth potential. The results of these efforts form the basis of training programs funded through the Center.

Training
Training opportunities are available through a variety of sources, including public schools, the Des Moines Area Community College, Drake University, and the Lincoln Technical Center. Courses offered have included Information Processing, Computer Literacy, and Basics of Supervision and Finance. Local unions also provide apprenticeship and pre-apprenticeship training, with programs having been

conducted in welding and highway sewer construction by union-provided instructors.

Supportive Services

In addition to training, Drake University offers deferred tuition to program participants for courses taken. As noted above, health care services for participants and their families are provided free of charge by the University of Osteopathic Medicine and Health Services. Child care and transportation services are also available.

Other Program Services

The Dislocated Worker Center offers pre-layoff assistance to companies and workers, including worker surveys, informational packages, planning and orientation meetings, one-to-one worker assistance and half-day group workshops. The involvement, from the beginning, of organized labor in the Center's efforts has resulted in greater participation among unionized plants in the pre-layoff assistance programs.

Results

Since the Center's inception in 1981, more than 1,000 dislocated workers and farmers have received reemployment assistance. For the 1983 program year, which ended June 30, 1984, there were 487 total participants, with 302 reemployed for a positive termination rate of 62 percent. And through the first three quarters of Program Year '84, 404 workers have received assistance from the Center. Of these, 175 have been reemployed, 284 have received pre-employment services and 120 have taken skill training courses.

For More Information, Contact:

Kris Zimmerman, Director/Region XI Dislocated Worker Center
United Way of Central Iowa
200 Walker, Suite B
Des Moines, Iowa 50317
(515) 282-5200

CREATIVE APPROACHES TO RETRAINING

LOCAL GOVERNMENT AS THE CATALYST FOR WORKER ASSISTANCE
Butte-Silver Bow, Montana

A combination of creative, resourceful public leadership and strongly committed private sector participation is the recipe for success in assisting dislocated workers in the city/county of Butte-Silver Bow, Montana. Necessitated by gradual and precipitous decline in the area's dominant industry, copper, an economic development strategy was developed with the enhancement of workers' existing skills as a main objective. The cooperative efforts of business, labor and public agencies, led by the local Chief Executive, have resulted thus far in three occupationally-tailored skills training programs targeted to impacted workers. A placement rate of nearly 75 percent attests to the success thus far of this small-city initiative in an area of limited economic growth.

Background

Since the early 1800's, copper has been king in the Butte-Silver Bow area. In this region of the country accustomed to boom-and-bust economic cycles, the seemingly irreversible decline of copper and related industries in recent years has presented conditions approximating economic disaster. The nadir of this decline was reached on July 1, 1983, when, six months after announcing its decision to close, the Anaconda Minerals Company suspended all copper mining activities in Butte-Silver Bow.

Added to other copper plant closings, which had begun around 1980, the Anaconda Mineral Company shutdown put more than 2,500 copper workers out of jobs. With "ripple" effects in the local economy caused by the closing, the jobless figure increased to more than 2,700— a number equivalent to 7.1 percent of the population. These losses placed the Butte-Silver Bow unemployment rate at roughly 10 percent.

Organizational Involvement and Funding

In response to the growing complexity of human and community problems emanating from the plant closings, the Chief Executive of the city/county government, Donald R. Peoples, launched an economic development plan in 1983 which involved the Anaconda Mineral Company and other local companies, organized labor and a number of public agencies. Though lacking financial resources to contribute to the plan's implementation, the local government has served as the catalyst for mobilizing local outside resources and coordinating activities. Joining in the efforts are the State Department of Labor, the Office of Public Instruction, and the State Vocational Education Program, as well as the Butte Job Service and the Butte Vocational Tech Center.

Funding for the three training initiatives has come from JTPA Title III funds—specifically, the DOL Secretary's Discretionary Fund, and the State of Montana Vocational Education Program. In-kind contributions have come from Anaconda Mineral Company, other local businesses and the Montana Power Company, as well as from the operating engineers', machinists and boilermakers', and electricians' unions and the Butte-Silver Bow Government. The table below summarizes all funding and sources of any kind of assistance:

Program Resources

Funding for the Operating Engineers Program

Cash

Department of Labor	$ 85,434

In-Kind Match

Anaconda Minerals Company Provided equipment, 2 instructors, 1 supervisor and training site	$ 813,982
Butte-Silver Bow Local Government Provided 2 instructors, equipment, paving materials, on-site training at stationary asphalt recycling plant	$ 134,082
Total	**$ 948,064**

Craft Skills Enhancement for Machinists & Boilermakers

Cash

Department of Labor	$ 68,296
State Education Office—Vocational Educational Development	$ 56,625

In-Kind Contribution

Anaconda/Arco Includes machine shop and equipment 1 supervisor, utilities, safety training and parts for diesel program	$5,115,000
Total	**$5,239,921**

Electrician—Instrumentation Technician

Cash

Department of Labor	$ 59,007
Education Office Vocational-Education	$ 13,427
In-Kind Contributions Anaconda/Arco, Montana Power Company, Mountain States Energy Includes instructors, supervisor, equipment, orientation and training.	$ 100,000
Total	**$ 172,434**

Characteristics of the Target Population

Indicative of the impact of a major industry shutdown on a small community, 95 percent of the target population had been employed by the Anaconda Minerals Company prior to July 1983. Characteristics of the population include: 99 percent males, 5.4 percent minority group members and 80 percent economically disadvantaged. In addition to the years of stable working experience which many of Butte's dislocated workers possess, a majority have high school diplomas (though eighth grade or lower levels of education are also present within the population).

Key Elements

The efforts of Butte-Silver Bow community on behalf of its dislocated worker population have come in the form of three Skill Enhancement Programs, the first two of which are currently operating, with the third beginning in the Fall of 1985. In designing each program, emphasis was placed on building upon the skills which workers already possess. Program planning sessions involving labor organizations, Anaconda Minerals Company and local officials have focused on identifying the skilled labor needs of local industries, including those which might facilitate resumption of the copper company's operations. The eligibility of participants for all programs was determined according to JTPA Title III criteria.

The Operating Engineers Program

The first of the three Skill Enhancement Programs was initiated in the Spring of 1984 and served 34 operating engineers. Limitations in the skills of these workers, who had been employed by the Anaconda Minerals Company, were identified by the local Operating Engineers Union (#375). Having operated only one type of mining industry equipment, these workers were ill-suited to compete for jobs in the general construction industry.

A four-month program was designed to train the 34 participants in the operation of seven pieces of commonly used, heavy construction equipment. The basics of slope-staking and grade reading were also taught, as well as the use of cutting torches and other tools. To facilitate training for this program, both Anaconda Minerals Company and the Butte-Silver Bow Government provided equipment and facilities, while the company also contributed the time and expertise of skill instructors. JTPA Title III Discretionary Funds were used to pay for additional instructors, training costs and supplies, supportive services, and training completion rewards.

The Machinists and Boilermakers Program

A second program to enhance workers' skills was launched in April 1985 for 40 machinists and boilermakers. As in the case of the operating engineers, these workers had acquired only limited skills through their copper industry jobs and were in need of upgrading.

A six-month program was designed for this group, focusing on skill attainment in machine tool operations, welding and diesel mechanics. As in the first program, Anaconda Mineral Company made available for the training its machine shops and equipment.

The Program For Electricians

A program to train 20 electricians in the fundamentals of instrumentation and control, electronic systems and equipment and pneumatic systems and equipment will begin in the Fall of 1985. This third dislocated worker initiative has been designed as a six-month course, and is intended to upgrade the skills and versatility of unemployed electricians. Resources for the program will come from JTPA and state Education Office funds, as well as in-kind contributions, including technical assistance, from the Montana Power Company, Mountain State Energy Company and Anaconda Minerals Company which has perhaps the most extensive facilities in the entire Northwest U.S. Also to be provided are instructors, parts for the diesel training component, and a training course in safety procedures. Funds for additional instructors came from the State Education Office, with JTPA funds covering supplies, insurance, needs-based payments and supportive services.

Results

Seventy-four percent of participants in the first Skill Enhancement Program, for operating engineers, were placed in jobs within ninety days of completing training. Of this 74 percent, 68 percent were placed with private industry employers. Only 1 program participant withdrew. While enrollees in the Machinists and Boilermakers Program are nearing completion of their training and the Electricians program is just beginning as of this writing, the results of the Operating Engineers Program offer the promise of success for these programs as well. A contributing factor to the enthusiasm for and success of that program is the close cooperation between the unions, Anaconda Minerals Company and local government agencies in the design and implementation of the training. Another is the cooperative spirit which existed among the workers themselves, exemplified in part by the participation of many workers as instructors in the training programs.

In contrast with the dislocated worker initiatives of other communities, the Butte-Silver Bow Skill Enhancement Programs have evolved without the establishment of a separate entity to plan and operate the programs. Rather, individually-designed and tailored training programs have been developed and targeted to specific segments of the workforce. The common concern and active partnership of the local government, organized labor and area industries are the key ingredients to this success story.

For More Information, Contact:

Donald R. Peoples, Chief Executive
Butte-Silver Bow
155 W. Granite Street
Butte, Montana 59701
(406) 723-8262

COMMON CONCERNS, COOPERATIVE SOLUTIONS

A TALE OF TWO CITIES
Eugene and Springfield, Oregon

With a county community college serving as the locus for training and reemployment assistance, two Oregon cities and surrounding areas are addressing the problems of worker dislocation brought on by decline/downturns in the region's dominant industry. Emphasizing the potential opportunities created by dislocation, the Lane Community College Dislocated Worker Program employs a holistic philosophy of linking career and life planning in its approach to reemployment rather than mere job search. At the heart of the Program is a flexible, customized approach to retraining tailored to emerging areas of occupational demand. For its efforts, the Program achieved an enviable placement rate of 87 percent in its first program year.

Background

Lane County, Oregon, encompassing the cities of Eugene and Springfield, has long been dependent on the lumber and wood products industry as the major source of employment and revenues. While the two cities serve also as centers of education, trade and services for the region, the economic dominance of the timber industry has been painfully asserted in recent years by job losses associated with the industry's decline.

Severe impacts were felt in the region due to the recession of 1980-82, during which unemployment in Lane County reached 12.5 percent, the highest on record for the county. Even as recovery from the recession was being declared nationally in 1983-84, the area's unemployment rate remained at least two percentage points above the national average. Between 1979-1982, nearly 4,000 jobs in the lumber and wood products industries disappeared. During the latter part of 1984 and early 1985, an additional 1,000 timber jobs were lost. The "ripple" effect of timber's decline has been felt throughout the area's economy, including at the county government level where one-third of the county's workforce has been laid off.

Organizational Involvement and Funding

Lane County's Dislocated Worker Program is a collaborative effort, operated by its community college in conjunction with the Eugene and Springfield JTPA Service delivery areas—the two SDA's have recently merged to create a single, joint entity—and two offices of the Oregon State Employment Service. The community college operates the program according to the terms of a performance-based contract drawn up by the area's Private Industry Council.

Program policies and overall direction are determined by an Advisory Task Force made up of representatives from the college, the SDA and the State Employment Service, with additional business, labor and community-based representation drawn from the PIC. In providing strong support for the Program, the governmental units of Lane County, and the cities of Eugene and Springfield have focused on developing contacts with their respective business communities and on linking the Program to overall economic development plans. Reflecting the views of his colleagues in Eugene and the county, Mayor John Lively of Springfield considers the responsibilities of the local officials involved to be those of resource brokers and overseers of the Program's performance. In view of the successes of the Dislocated Worker Program to date, no operational role for the local government has been considered necessary.

Funding for Lane Community College Program has come from both formula Title III funds and national discretionary Title III funds under JTPA. For the 1984 program year, the dual-community initiative received $350,000 in formula funds and $500,000 in discretionary funds. The matching share requirement for the use of Title III funds has been partially offset by the amount of the program's performance which exceeds the terms of the performance contract—an innovative approach to the matching requirements. Other in-kind contributions have come from area businesses, mainly in the form of materials, equipment and/or facilities. One example of this was the contribution of $5,000 by a local software company toward a dental office management training program. The program is currently funded at $100,000, due primarily to its initial success.

Characteristics of the Target Population

The widespread effects of downturns in the timber industries are also reflected in the makeup of the Program's target population. While sizable layoffs have occurred in two of the area's largest employers, Weyerhauser and Champion International, the ranks of dislocated workers have swollen from layoffs in small, and medium-sized companies of different types as well. Thus, the population of dislocated workers reflects a diverse mix of young and old, blue collar and white collar, and highly skilled and unskilled individuals.

In addition to its diversity, the target population presents some unique challenges to the architects of the Dislocated Worker Program. These challenges, owing to characteristics of the population and the area's economy, derive from: (1) a strong work ethic and suspicion of government handouts on the part of Oregonians; (2) an urgent need to re-enter the labor force quickly in order to maintain traditionally stable incomes; (3) the realization that many workers will have to make major career shift; and (4) the lack of opportunities for extensive, long-term retraining.

Key Elements

The Lane Community College Program is a multifaceted dislocated worker initiative, combining assistance for self-directed job search with skill upgrading and customized training. Confidence building, positive attitude counseling and a holistic life-career planning approach complement the job search and training components. Key elements of the Program are:

Recruitment and Certification
These functions are performed by the Oregon State Employment Service through the work of three loaned employment service specialists. This arrangement has enabled the Program to access a network of employment service information on growth occupations and company-specific opportunities.

Assessment
Following certification by the state Employment Service, participants are referred to Lane Community College for assessment and determination of service needs. A

computerized occupational assessment system is used to ascertain career/life interests and employability, after which a training plan is developed if needed.

Job Search Assistance

All program participants take part in an extensive job search workshop which runs for up to eight full days. In groups of fifteen to twenty persons, participants play active roles, making presentations and conducting research needed for identifying job possibilities. Through these workshops, which lead to the formation of job clubs, participants gain valuable knowledge about career/life planning—as opposed to basic job hunting—and emerge from the workshops with a strong sense of support and camaraderie.

Training Services

Upgrading training in both basic and specialized skill areas is available through the Community College; approximately 60 percent of the Program's participants enroll in one form or the other. Training has been offered in such fields as word processing and micro-computers and sales techniques.

An important feature of the Program is its outreach to local employers in order to identify in-demand occupations. Based on identified needs, innovative, customized training programs are then designed and implemented. Among the customized programs which have been conducted are: the dental office management course, a six-month program in electro-mechanical maintenance, ophthalmological assistant training in conjunction with a pioneering laser surgery company, and a mini-course in outside industrial sales. About one-third of the training recipients are placed through OJT contracts with employers.

Placement

Two full-time Employment/Marketing Specialists work to place participants and create visibility for the Program through presentations to community and business groups. Visibility is also gained through newspaper ads, public service announcements, community employment forums, and—beginning in March of 1985—a program newsletter published for participants and prospective employers. The Employment/Marketing Specialists also maintain close contact with area economic development agencies.

Entrepreneurial Assistance

A distinctive feature of the Dislocated Worker Program is its tie to the area's Business Assistance Center which is also affiliated with the community college. Through this tie, program participants who wish to enter business for themselves are given a full range of orientation in marketing, taxes, business accounting and business plan preparation. The Program also provides up to $500 to assist with business start-up costs. Thus far, 7 participants have started businesses ranging from housecleaning services to landscaping to business consulting.

Results

In its first year of operations, 1983, the Lane Community College Dislocated Worker Program placed 130 of 150 participants—87 percent—in jobs. In 1984, the Program served 400 persons, 225 of whom have found employment in various occupations. The continued success of the Program is credited to its flexibility, its performance-driven contractual basis and to its positive holistic philosophy toward the potential for finding satisfying career/life opportunities.

For More Information Contact:

Nan Poppe, Program Coordinator
Lane Community College Dislocated
   Worker Program
4000 East 30th Avenue
Eugene, Oregon 97405
(503) 726-2223